p es and tarts

100 EASY RECIPES
pies and tarts

bay books

contents

savoury pies

family-style meat pie

1 tablespoon oil
1 onion, chopped
1 garlic clove, crushed
750 g (1 lb 10 oz) minced (ground) beef
250 ml (9 fl oz/1 cup) beef stock
250 ml (9 fl oz/1 cup) beer
1 tablespoon tomato paste
   (concentrated purée)
1 tablespoon yeast extract (Marmite)
1 tablespoon worcestershire sauce
2 teaspoons cornflour (cornstarch)
375 g (13 oz) shortcrust pastry
375 g (13 oz) ready-made puff pastry
1 egg, lightly beaten, to glaze

serves 6

method   Heat the oil in a large saucepan over medium heat and cook the onion for 5 minutes, until golden. Increase the heat, add the garlic and beef and cook, breaking up any lumps, for 5 minutes, or until the beef changes colour.

Add the stock, beer, tomato paste, yeast extract, worcestershire sauce and 125 ml (4 fl oz/½ cup) water. Reduce the heat to medium and cook for 1 hour, or until there is little liquid left. Combine the cornflour with 1 tablespoon water, then stir it into the meat and cook for 5 minutes, or until thick and glossy. Remove from the heat and cool completely.

Lightly grease an 18 cm (7 inch) pie tin. Roll out the shortcrust pastry between two sheets of baking paper until large enough to line the base and side of the tin. Use a small ball of pastry to help press the pastry into the tin, allowing any excess to hang over the side.

Roll out the puff pastry between two sheets of baking paper to make a 23 cm (9 inch) circle. Spoon the filling into the pastry shell and smooth it down. Brush the pastry edges with the egg, then place the puff pastry over the top. Cut off any excess with a sharp knife. Press the top and bottom pastries together, then scallop the edges with a fork or your fingers. Refrigerate for 20 minutes. Preheat the oven to 200°C (400°F/Gas 6) and heat a baking tray.

Brush the remaining egg over the top of the pie, place on the hot tray on the bottom shelf of the oven and bake for 25–30 minutes, or until golden and well puffed.

low-fat spinach pie

1.5 kg (3 lb 5 oz) English spinach
2 teaspoons olive oil
1 onion, chopped
4 spring onions (scallions), chopped
750 g (1 lb 10 oz/3 cups) reduced-fat
cottage cheese
2 eggs, lightly beaten
2 garlic cloves, crushed
pinch of ground nutmeg
3 tablespoons chopped mint
8 sheets filo pastry
30 g (1 oz) butter, melted
40 g (1½ oz/½ cup) fresh breadcrumbs

serves 6

method Preheat the oven to 180°C (350°F/Gas 4) and lightly spray a 1.5 litre (52 fl oz/6 cup) ovenproof dish with oil. Trim and wash the spinach leaves, then place in a large saucepan with the water clinging to the leaves. Cover and cook for 2–3 minutes, or until just wilted. Drain, cool, then squeeze dry and chop.

Heat the oil in a small pan. Add the onion and spring onion and cook for 2–3 minutes, until softened. Combine in a bowl with the chopped spinach. Stir in the cottage cheese, egg, garlic, nutmeg and mint. Season and mix thoroughly.

Brush a sheet of filo pastry with a little butter. Fold in half widthways and line the base and sides of the dish. Repeat with three more sheets. Keep the unused sheets moist by covering with a damp tea towel (dish towel).

Sprinkle the breadcrumbs over the pastry. Spread the filling into the dish. Fold over any overlapping pastry. Brush and fold another sheet and place on top. Repeat with three more sheets. Tuck the pastry in at the sides. Brush the top with any remaining butter. Score squares or diamonds on the top using a sharp knife.

Bake for 40 minutes, or until golden. Cut into squares to serve.

bacon and egg pie

1 sheet shortcrust pastry
2 teaspoons oil
4 bacon slices, chopped
5 eggs, lightly beaten
60 ml (2 fl oz/¼ cup) cream
1 sheet puff pastry
1 egg, lightly beaten, to glaze

serves 4–6

method Preheat the oven to 210°C (415°F/Gas 6–7). Lightly oil a 20 cm (8 inch) loose-based flan (tart) tin. Place the shortcrust pastry in the tin and trim the pastry edges. Cut a sheet of baking paper to cover the pastry-lined tin. Spread a layer of baking beads, dried beans or rice over the paper. Bake for 10 minutes and then discard the paper and rice. Bake the pastry for another 5–10 minutes, or until golden. Allow to cool.

Heat the oil in a frying pan. Add the bacon and cook over medium heat for a few minutes, or until lightly browned. Drain on paper towel and allow to cool slightly. Arrange the bacon over the pastry base and pour the mixed eggs and cream over the top.

Brush the edges of the pastry with the egg glaze, cover with puff pastry and press on firmly to seal. Trim the pastry edges and decorate the top with trimmings. Brush with remaining egg glaze and bake for 40 minutes, or until puffed and golden brown.

moroccan lamb pie

60 ml (2 fl oz/¼ cup) olive oil
2 onions, finely chopped
4 garlic cloves, crushed
1¼ teaspoons each ground cinnamon,
cumin and coriander
½ teaspoon ground ginger
large pinch of cayenne pepper
1.2 kg (2 lb 10 oz) boned lamb leg,
cut into small cubes
375 ml (13 fl oz/1½ cups) chicken stock
2 teaspoons grated lemon zest
1 tablespoon lemon juice
2 carrots, cut into small cubes
60 g (2¼ oz/½ cup) ground almonds
3 large handfuls coriander (cilantro)
leaves, chopped
500 g (1 lb 2 oz) ready-made puff pastry
1 egg, lightly beaten, to glaze

serves 6–8

method   Heat the oil in a large saucepan. Add the onion, garlic and spices and cook, stirring, over medium heat for 40 seconds. Add the lamb and stir until coated. Add the stock, lemon zest and juice and cook, covered, over low heat for 45 minutes. Add the carrot. Simmer, covered, for 45 minutes. Stir in the almonds. Boil for 30 minutes, until the sauce becomes very thick. Stir in the chopped coriander, season and cool.

Preheat the oven to 200°C (400°F/Gas 6) and heat a baking tray. Grease a 20 cm (8 inch) pie dish. Roll out the pastry to a 40 cm (16 inch) round and neaten the edge. Line the dish, leaving the pastry overhanging the rim. Spoon in the filling and level the surface. Fold the overhanging pastry into loose pleats over the filling. Using scissors, cut out Vs of pastry where it falls into deep folds so the pastry can bake evenly.

Brush with egg and bake on the hot tray in the centre of the oven for 20 minutes. Reduce the oven to 180°C (350°F/Gas 4), cover the pie with foil and bake for another 20 minutes.

chicken and leek pie

60 g (2 oz) butter
2 large leeks, white part only, finely sliced
4 spring onions (scallions), sliced
1 garlic clove, crushed
30 g (1 oz/¼ cup) plain (all-purpose) flour
375 ml (13 fl oz/1½ cups) chicken stock
125 ml (4 fl oz/½ cup) cream
1 barbecued chicken, skin and bones removed, chopped
2 sheets puff pastry
60 ml (2 fl oz/¼ cup) milk

serves 4–6

method   Preheat the oven to 200°C (400°F/Gas 6). In a large saucepan, melt the butter and add the leek, spring onion and garlic. Cook over low heat for 6 minutes, or until the leek is soft but not browned. Sprinkle in the flour and mix well. Pour in the stock gradually and cook, stirring well, until thick and smooth. Stir in the cream and add the chicken. Put the mixture in a shallow 20 cm (8 inch) pie dish and set aside to cool.

Cut a circle out of one of the sheets of pastry to cover the top of the pie. Paint around the rim of the pie dish with a little of the milk. Put the pastry on top and seal around the edge firmly. Trim off any overhanging pastry and decorate the edge with a fork.

Cut the other sheet of pastry into 1 cm (½ inch) strips and loosely roll up each strip into a spiral. Arrange the spirals on top of the pie, leaving gaps between them. The spirals may not cover the whole surface of the pie. Make a few small holes between the spirals to let out any steam and brush the top of the pie lightly with the remaining milk. Bake for 35–40 minutes, or until the top of the pie is brown and crispy. Make sure the spirals are well cooked and are not raw in the middle.

filo vegetable strudel

1 large eggplant (aubergine), thinly sliced
1 red capsicum (pepper)
3 zucchini (courgettes), sliced lengthways
2 tablespoons olive oil
6 sheets filo pastry
50 g (2 oz) baby English spinach leaves
60 g (2 oz) feta cheese, sliced

serves 6–8

method Preheat the oven to 190°C (375°F/Gas 5). Sprinkle the eggplant slices with a little salt and leave to drain in a colander for 30 minutes. Pat dry with paper towels.

Cut the capsicum into quarters and place, skin side up, under a hot grill (broiler) for 10 minutes, or until the skin blackens. Put the capsicum pieces in a plastic bag and leave to cool. Peel away the skin. Brush the eggplant and zucchini with olive oil and grill for 5–10 minutes, or until golden brown. Leave to cool.

Brush one sheet of filo pastry at a time with olive oil, then place them on top of each other. Place half of the eggplant slices lengthways down the centre of the filo and top with a layer of zucchini, capsicum, spinach and feta cheese. Repeat the layers until all the vegetables and cheese are used. Tuck in the ends of the pastry, then roll up like a parcel. Brush lightly with olive oil and place on a baking tray. Bake for 35 minutes, or until golden brown.

note *Unopened packets of filo pastry can be stored in the fridge for up to a month. Once opened, use within 2–3 days.*

shepherd's pie

60 ml (2 fl oz/¼ cup) olive oil
1 large onion, finely chopped
2 garlic cloves, crushed
2 celery stalks, finely chopped
3 carrots, diced
2 bay leaves
1 tablespoon thyme, chopped
1 kg (2 lb 4 oz) minced (ground) lamb
1½ tablespoons plain (all-purpose) flour
125 ml (4 fl oz/½ cup) dry red wine
2 tablespoons tomato paste
   (concentrated purée)
400 g (14 oz) tinned chopped tomatoes
800 g (1 lb 12 oz) potatoes, chopped
60 ml (2 fl oz/¼ cup) milk
100 g (4 oz) butter
½ teaspoon ground nutmeg

serves 6

method Heat 2 tablespoons of the oil in a large, heavy-based saucepan and cook the onion for 3–4 minutes, or until softened. Add the garlic, celery, carrot, bay leaves and chopped thyme, and cook for 2–3 minutes. Transfer to a bowl and remove the bay leaves.

Add the remaining oil to the pan and cook the lamb over high heat for 5–6 minutes, or until it changes colour. Mix in the flour, cook for 1 minute, then pour in the red wine and cook for 2–3 minutes. Return all the vegetables to the pan with the tomato paste and tomato. Reduce the heat, cover and simmer for 45 minutes, stirring occasionally. Season and transfer to a shallow 3 litre (12 cup) casserole dish and leave to cool. Preheat the oven to 180°C (350°F/Gas 4).

Boil the potatoes in salted water for 20–25 minutes, or until tender. Drain, then mash with the milk and butter until smooth. Season with nutmeg and black pepper. Spoon over the mince and fluff with a fork. Bake for 40 minutes, until golden and crusty.

100 EASY RECIPES PIES AND TARTS

cheese and onion pie

2 tablespoons olive oil
2 onions, chopped
185 g (7 oz/1½ cups) grated cheddar cheese
1 tablespoon chopped flat-leaf (Italian) parsley
1 teaspoon English mustard
2 teaspoons worcestershire sauce
2 eggs, beaten
2 sheets puff pastry

serves 4

method Preheat the oven to 190°C (375°F/Gas 5). Heat the oil in a large frying pan over medium heat, add the onion and cook for 5–7 minutes, or until soft and golden. Transfer to a bowl and allow to cool for 10 minutes.

Add the cheese, parsley, mustard and worcestershire sauce to the onion and mix well. Add half the egg to the bowl and season well.

Cut each sheet of pastry into a 23 cm (9 inch) circle. Lay one sheet of pastry on a lined baking tray. Spread the filling over the pastry base, piling it higher in the middle and leaving a narrow border. Lightly brush the border with some of the remaining egg and put the second sheet on top, stretching it slightly to fit. Press and seal the edges well and brush the top with the remaining egg. Cut two slits in the top for steam holes.

Bake for 10 minutes, then reduce the heat to 180°C (350°F/Gas 4) and cook for another 20–25 minutes, or until the pastry is crisp and golden brown.

welsh lamb pie

750 g (1 lb 10 oz) boned lamb shoulder, cubed
90 g (3 oz/¾ cup) plain (all-purpose) flour,
    seasoned
2 tablespoons olive oil
200 g (7 oz) bacon slices, finely chopped
2 garlic cloves, chopped
4 large leeks, white part only, sliced
1 large carrot, chopped
2 large potatoes, peeled and diced
310 ml (11 fl oz/1¼ cups) beef stock
1 bay leaf
2 teaspoons chopped parsley
375 g (13 oz) ready-made flaky pastry
1 egg, lightly beaten, to glaze

serves 6

method   Toss the meat in the flour. Heat the oil in a large frying pan over medium heat and brown the meat in batches for 4–5 minutes, then remove from the pan. Cook the bacon for 3 minutes. Add the garlic and leek and cook for 5 minutes, or until soft.

Put the meat in a large saucepan, add the leek and bacon, carrot, potato, stock and bay leaf and bring to the boil, then reduce the heat, cover and simmer for 30 minutes. Uncover and simmer for 1 hour, or until the meat is cooked and the liquid has thickened. Season to taste. Remove the bay leaf, stir in the parsley and set aside to cool.

Preheat the oven to 200°C (400°F/Gas 6). Spoon the filling into an 18 cm (7 inch) pie dish. Roll out the pastry between two sheets of baking paper until large enough to cover the pie. Trim the edges and pinch to seal.

Decorate the pie with pastry trimmings. Cut two slits in the top for steam to escape. Brush with egg and bake for 45 minutes, or until the pastry is crisp and golden.

salmon pie

60 g (2 oz) butter
1 onion, finely chopped
200 g (7 oz) button mushrooms, sliced
2 tablespoons lemon juice
220 g (8 oz) salmon fillet, boned,
skinned and cubed
2 hard-boiled eggs, chopped
2 tablespoons chopped dill
2 tablespoons chopped parsley
185 g (7 oz/1 cup) cooked rice
60 ml (2 fl oz/¼ cup) cream
375 g (13 oz) ready-made puff pastry
1 egg, lightly beaten, to glaze

serves 4–6

method Lightly brush a baking tray with oil. Melt half the butter in a frying pan and cook the onion for 5 minutes, or until soft but not browned. Add the mushrooms and cook for 5 minutes. Stir in the lemon juice and transfer to a bowl.

Melt the remaining butter in the same pan, add the salmon and cook for 2 minutes. Remove from the heat, cool slightly and add the egg, dill, parsley, salt and pepper. Stir gently and set aside. Stir together the rice and cream.

Roll out half the pastry to a rectangle measuring 18 x 30 cm (7 x 12 inches) and place on the baking tray. Spread with half the rice mixture, leaving a small border all the way around. Top with the salmon mixture, then the mushroom mixture, and finish with the remaining rice.

Roll out the remaining pastry to 20 x 33 cm (8 x 13 inches) to cover the filling. Crimp the edges to seal. Refrigerate for 30 minutes. Preheat the oven to 210°C (415°F/Gas 6–7). Brush with the egg and bake for 15 minutes. Reduce the heat to 180°C (350°F/Gas 4) and bake for a further 15–20 minutes until golden.

veal, jerusalem artichoke and potato pie

1 tablespoon olive oil
500 g (1 lb 2 oz) lean minced (ground) veal
2 onions, finely chopped
3 garlic cloves, crushed
150 g (5 oz) bacon, diced
½ teaspoon dried rosemary
2 tablespoons plain (all-purpose) flour
pinch of cayenne pepper
125 ml (4 fl oz/½ cup) dry white wine
150 ml (5 fl oz) cream
1 egg, lightly beaten
2 hard-boiled eggs, roughly chopped

topping

500 g (1 lb 2 oz) Jerusalem artichokes
400 g (14 oz) potatoes
100 g (4 oz) butter

serves 4–6

method   Heat the oil in a large frying pan and cook the veal, onion, garlic, bacon and rosemary, stirring often, for 10 minutes, or until the veal changes colour. Stir in the flour and cayenne pepper and cook for 1 minute. Pour in the wine and 125 ml (4 fl oz/½ cup) water. Season well. Simmer for 5 minutes, or until the sauce is very thick, then stir in the cream, beaten egg and chopped egg.

Preheat the oven to 210°C (415°F/Gas 6–7). Lightly grease a 20 cm (8 inch) spring-form tin. Peel and chop the artichokes and potatoes and boil together for 12–15 minutes, until tender. Drain, add the butter, then mash until smooth.

Spoon the filling into the tin then spread with the topping. Bake for 20 minutes, then reduce the heat to 180°C (350°F/Gas 4) and bake for another 30 minutes, or until golden on top.

cornish pasties

310 g (11 oz/2½ cups) plain (all-purpose) flour
125 g (4½ oz) butter, chilled and cubed
80–100 ml (3–4 fl oz) iced water
160 g (5 oz) round steak, diced
1 small potato, finely chopped
1 small onion, finely chopped
1 small carrot, finely chopped
1–2 teaspoons worcestershire sauce
2 tablespoons beef stock
1 egg, lightly beaten, to glaze

makes 6

method   Grease a baking tray. Process the flour, butter and a pinch of salt in a food processor for 15 seconds, or until crumbly. Add the water and process in short bursts until it comes together. Turn out onto a floured surface and form into a ball. Wrap in plastic and chill for 30 minutes. Preheat the oven to 210°C (415°F/Gas 6–7).

Mix together the steak, potato, onion, carrot, worcestershire sauce and stock. Season well.

Divide the dough into six portions and roll out to 3 mm (1/8 inch) thick. Cut into six 16 cm (6¼ inch) rounds. Divide the filling evenly and put in the centre of each pastry circle.

Brush the pastry edges with the egg and fold over. Pinch to form a frill and place on the tray. Brush with the remaining egg and bake for 15 minutes. Lower the heat to 180°C (350°F/Gas 4) and bake for a further 25–30 minutes, or until golden.

fisherman's pie

800 g (1 lb 12 oz) white fish fillets
375 ml (13 fl oz/1½ cups) milk
1 onion, chopped
2 cloves
50 g (2 oz) butter
2 tablespoons plain (all-purpose) flour
pinch of ground nutmeg
2 tablespoons chopped parsley
150 g (5 oz/1 cup) peas
750 g (1 lb 10 oz) potatoes, quartered
2 tablespoons hot milk
30 g (1 oz/¼ cup) grated cheddar cheese

serves 4

method   Place the fish in a wide pan and cover with the milk. Add the onion and cloves and bring to the boil. Reduce the heat and simmer for 5 minutes, or until the fish is cooked and flakes easily with a fork.

Preheat the oven to 180°C (350°F/Gas 4). Remove the fish from the pan, reserving the milk and onion. Discard the cloves. Allow the fish to cool then remove any bones and flake the flesh into bite-sized pieces with a fork.

Heat half the butter in a pan, stir in the flour and cook, stirring, for 1 minute. Slowly add the reserved milk, stirring constantly until smooth. Cook, stirring, until the sauce begins to bubble, then cook for another minute. Remove from the heat, cool slightly, then add the nutmeg, parsley and peas. Season and gently fold in the fish. Spoon into a 1.25 litre (5 cup) casserole.

Cook the potatoes in a pan of boiling water until tender. Drain and add the hot milk and remaining butter. Mash until very smooth. Add the cheese. If the mash is very stiff add a little more milk, but it should be fairly firm.

Spoon the potato over the top and rough up with a fork, or spoon the potato into a piping bag and neatly pipe over the top. Bake for 45 minutes, until the potato begins to brown.

italian zucchini pie

310 g (11 oz/2½ cups) plain (all-purpose) flour
80 ml (3 fl oz/⅓ cup) olive oil
1 egg, beaten
3–4 tablespoons iced water
600 g (1 lb 5 oz) zucchini (courgettes)
150 g (5 oz) provolone cheese, grated
120 g (4 oz/½ cup) ricotta cheese
3 eggs
2 garlic cloves, crushed
2 teaspoons finely chopped basil
pinch of ground nutmeg
1 egg, lightly beaten, to glaze

serves 6

method Sift the flour and ½ teaspoon salt into a large bowl and make a well. Combine the oil, egg and almost all the water and add to the flour. Mix with a flat-bladed knife until the mixture forms beads. Add water if needed. Gather into a ball, wrap in plastic and refrigerate for 30 minutes.

Preheat the oven to 200°C (400°F/Gas 6) and heat a baking tray. Grease an 18 cm (7 inch) pie dish. Grate the zucchini, toss with ¼ teaspoon salt and drain in a colander for 30 minutes. Squeeze out any liquid and place the zucchini in a large bowl with the provolone, ricotta, eggs, garlic, basil and nutmeg. Season well and mix thoroughly.

Roll out two-thirds of the pastry between two sheets of baking paper until large enough to line the base and side of the dish. Spoon the filling into the pastry shell and level the surface. Brush the pastry rim with egg. Roll out two-thirds of the remaining dough between the baking paper to make a lid. Cover the filling and press the edges together firmly. Trim and crimp the rim. Prick the top all over with a skewer and brush with egg.

Roll the remaining dough into a 30 x 10 cm (12 x 4 inch) long strip. Use a long sharp knife to cut this into nine 1 cm (½ inch) wide lengths. Press three ropes together at one end and then press them onto the work surface to secure them. Plait the ropes and make two more plaits. Trim the ends and space the plaits parallel across the centre of the pie. Brush with egg. Bake on the hot tray for 50 minutes, or until the pastry is golden.

beef and red wine pies

60 ml (2 fl oz/¼ cup) oil
1.5 kg (3 lb 5 oz) chuck steak, cubed
2 onions, chopped
1 garlic clove, crushed
30 g (1 oz/¼ cup) plain (all-purpose) flour
310 ml (11 fl oz/1¼ cups) dry red wine
500 ml (17 fl oz/2 cups) beef stock
2 bay leaves
2 thyme sprigs
2 carrots, chopped
4 sheets shortcrust pastry
1 egg, lightly beaten
4 sheets puff pastry

makes 6

method   Heat 2 tablespoons of oil in a large frying pan and fry the meat in batches until browned. Remove all the meat from the pan. Heat the remaining oil in the same pan, add the onion and garlic and cook, stirring, until golden brown. Add the flour and stir over medium heat for 2 minutes, or until well browned.

Remove from the heat and gradually stir in the combined wine and stock. Return to the heat and stir until the mixture boils and thickens. Return the meat to the pan with the bay leaves and thyme, and simmer for 1 hour. Add the carrot and simmer for another 45 minutes, until the meat and carrot are tender and the sauce has thickened. Season to taste, and remove the bay leaves and thyme. Cool.

Preheat the oven to 200°C (400°F/Gas 6) and lightly grease six 9 cm (3½ inch) metal pie tins. Cut the shortcrust pastry sheets in half diagonally. Line the base and side of each pie tin with the pastry and trim the edges. Line each pie with baking paper and fill with baking beads. Place on a baking tray and bake for 8 minutes. Remove the paper and beads and bake for a further 8 minutes, or until the pastry is lightly browned. Cool.

Spoon the filling into the pastry cases and brush the edges with some of the beaten egg. Cut the puff pastry sheets in half diagonally and cover the tops of the pies. Trim the excess, pressing the edges with a fork to seal. Cut a slit in the top of each pie. Brush the tops with egg, and bake for 20–25 minutes, or until the pastry is golden brown.

sweet potato, pumpkin and coconut pies

2 tablespoons oil
1 onion, finely chopped
2 garlic cloves, crushed
1 teaspoon grated ginger
1 small red chilli, chopped
250 g (9 oz) orange sweet potato, peeled and cubed
250 g (9 oz) pumpkin, peeled and cubed
½ teaspoon fennel seeds
½ teaspoon mustard seeds
½ teaspoon ground turmeric
½ teaspoon ground cumin
150 ml (5 fl oz) tinned coconut milk
3 tablespoons chopped coriander (cilantro) leaves
4 sheets puff pastry
1 egg yolk, to glaze

makes 8

method Heat the oil in a pan and cook the onion, garlic, ginger and chilli for 5 minutes, stirring continuously, until the onion is cooked. Add the sweet potato, pumpkin, fennel and mustard seeds, turmeric and cumin. Stir for 2 minutes, then add the coconut milk and 2 tablespoons of water. Cook over low heat for 20 minutes, stirring frequently, or until the vegetables are tender. Stir through the coriander and let cool.

Preheat the oven to 190°C (375°F/Gas 5). Grease a baking tray. Cut out eight 9 cm (3½ inch) circles from two sheets of the pastry. Place them on the tray and divide the filling between them, spreading it to within 1 cm (½ inch) of the edge. Mound the filling slightly. Brush the edges of the pastry with a little water.

Use a lattice cutter or sharp knife to cut out eight 10 cm (4 inch) circles from the remaining pastry. Carefully open out the lattices and fit them over the mixture. Press the edges together firmly to seal. Using the back of a knife, press the outside edge lightly at 1 cm (½ inch) intervals. Refrigerate for at least 20 minutes.

Mix the egg yolk with a little water. Brush the pastry. Bake for 20–25 minutes, until golden.

ham and chicken pie

375 g (13 oz/3 cups) plain (all-purpose) flour
180 g (6 oz) butter, chilled and cubed
2–3 tablespoons iced water
1 egg, lightly beaten

filling

1 kg (2 lb 4 oz) minced (ground) chicken
1 teaspoon dried mixed herbs
2 eggs, lightly beaten
3 spring onions (scallions), finely chopped
2 tablespoons chopped parsley
2 teaspoons French mustard
80 ml (3 fl oz/⅓ cup) cream
200 g (7 oz) sliced leg ham

serves 8–10

method Preheat the oven to 180°C (350°F/Gas 4). Mix the flour and butter in a food processor for 20 seconds or until fine and crumbly. Add the water and process for another 20 seconds, or until the mixture comes together. Turn onto a lightly floured surface and press together until smooth. Roll out two-thirds of the pastry to line a 20 cm (8 inch) spring-form tin, leaving some pastry hanging over the side. Cover with plastic wrap and refrigerate until required. Wrap the remaining pastry in plastic wrap and refrigerate.

To make the filling, mix together the chicken, mixed herbs, egg, spring onion, parsley, mustard and cream and season well.

Spoon a third of the filling into the pastry-lined tin and smooth the surface. Top with half the ham and then another chicken layer, followed by the remaining ham and then a final layer of chicken filling.

Brush around the inside edge of pastry with egg. Roll out the remaining pastry to make the pie lid, pressing the pastry edges together. Trim the edge. Decorate the top with pastry trimmings. Brush with beaten egg and bake for 1 hour, or until golden brown.

creamy snapper pies

2 tablespoons olive oil
4 onions, thinly sliced
375 ml (13 fl oz/1½ cups) fish stock
875 ml (30 fl oz/3½ cups) cream
1 kg (2 lb 4 oz) skinless snapper fillets,
cut into bite-sized pieces
2 sheets puff pastry
1 egg, lightly beaten, to glaze

makes 6

method Preheat the oven to 220°C (425°F/Gas 7). Heat the oil in a large saucepan, add the onion and stir over medium heat for 20 minutes, or until golden brown and slightly caramelised.

Add the stock, bring to the boil and cook for 10 minutes, or until the liquid has nearly evaporated. Stir in the cream, bring to the boil, then simmer for 20 minutes, until the liquid reduces by half or coats the back of a spoon.

Divide half the sauce among six 310 ml (11 fl oz/1¼ cup) deep ovenproof dishes. Put some fish in each dish and top with the sauce.

Cut the pastry into rounds slightly larger than the tops of the dishes. Brush the edges of the pastry with a little of the egg. Press onto the dishes. Brush lightly with the remaining egg. Bake for 30 minutes, or until the pastry is crisp, golden and puffed.

potato and goat's cheese pies

4 potatoes, peeled
4 slices prosciutto
150 g (5 oz) goat's cheese
250 g (9 oz/1 cup) sour cream
2 eggs, lightly beaten
125 ml (4 fl oz/½ cup) cream

makes 4

method Brush four 250 ml (9 fl oz/1 cup) ramekins with melted butter. Preheat the oven to 180°C (350°F/Gas 4).

For each pie, thinly slice a potato and pat dry with paper towel. Line the base of a ramekin with a half slice of prosciutto. Layer half the potato slices neatly into the dishes. Put the other half slice of prosciutto on top and crumble a quarter of the goat's cheese over it. Cover with the remaining potato slices and press down firmly. The potato should fill the dish to the top.

Mix together the sour cream, egg and cream and season well. Pour into the ramekins, allowing it to seep through the layers. Place on a baking tray and bake for 50–60 minutes, or until the potato is soft when tested with a skewer. Leave for 5 minutes, then run a knife around the edge and turn out onto serving plates.

brik a l'oeuf

6 sheets filo pastry
30 g (1 oz) butter, melted
1 small onion, finely chopped
200 g (7 oz) tinned tuna in oil, drained
6 pitted black olives, chopped
1 tablespoon chopped parsley
2 eggs

makes 2

method Preheat the oven to 200°C (400°F/Gas 6). Cut the pastry sheets in half widthways. Brush four sheets with melted butter and lay them on top of each other. Place half of the combined onion, tuna, olives and parsley at one end and make a well in the centre. Break an egg into the well, being careful to leave the yolk whole. Season well.

Brush two more sheets with melted butter, place them together and lay them on top of the tuna and egg. Fold in the sides and roll up to form a neat firm package, still keeping the egg whole. Place on a baking tray and brush with some melted butter. Repeat with the remaining pastry and filling. Bake for 20 minutes, or until golden.

note *The yolk will still be soft after 20 minutes of cooking. If you prefer a firmer egg, bake for longer. Tuna in oil is preferable to brine as it will keep the filling moist when cooked.*

chicken coriander pie

50 g (2 oz) butter
2 onions, chopped
100 g (4 oz) button mushrooms, sliced
250 g (9 oz) cooked chicken, chopped
4 hard-boiled eggs
1 tablespoon plain (all-purpose) flour
280 ml (10 fl oz) chicken stock
1 egg yolk
3 tablespoons chopped coriander
   (cilantro) leaves
250 g (8 oz) ready-made puff pastry
1 egg, lightly beaten, to glaze

serves 4

method Melt half the butter in a large pan. Add the onion and mushrooms and cook for 5 minutes, or until soft, then stir in the chicken. Spoon half the mixture into a 20 cm (8 inch) round, straight-sided pie dish. Slice the eggs and lay over the chicken, then top with the remaining mixture.

Preheat the oven to 200°C (400°F/Gas 6). Melt the remaining butter in a saucepan, add the flour and cook for 1 minute. Gradually add the stock and cook for 4 minutes, stirring constantly, then remove from the heat. Stir in the egg yolk and coriander and season. Leave to cool, then pour over the chicken filling in the pie dish.

Roll out the pastry into a square larger than the pie dish. Dampen the rim with water and lay the pastry over the top, pressing down firmly to seal. Trim the edges. Roll the leftover pastry into a long strip. Slice it into three equal lengths and make a plait. Brush the pie with egg and place the plait around the edge. Brush with the remaining egg. Make a few slits in the centre and bake for 35 minutes, until golden.

lamb and filo pie

2 tablespoons oil
2 onions, chopped
1 garlic clove, chopped
1 teaspoon ground cumin
1 teaspoon ground coriander
½ teaspoon ground cinnamon
1 kg (2 lb 4 oz) minced (ground) lamb
3 tablespoons chopped parsley
2 tablespoons chopped mint
1 tablespoon tomato paste
(concentrated purée)
10 sheets filo pastry
250 g (9 oz) unsalted butter, melted

serves 6

method Heat the oil in a large frying pan and cook the onion and garlic for 3 minutes, or until just soft. Add the cumin, coriander and cinnamon, and cook, stirring, for 1 minute.

Add the minced lamb to the pan and cook over medium–high heat for 10 minutes or until the meat is brown and the liquid has evaporated. Use a fork to break up any lumps. Add the fresh herbs, tomato paste and a little salt and mix well. Set aside to cool.

Preheat the oven to 180°C (350°F/Gas 4) and lightly grease a 33 x 23 cm (13 x 9 inch) ovenproof dish with butter or oil. Remove 3 sheets of filo and cover the rest with a damp tea towel (dish towel) to prevent them drying out. Brush one sheet of pastry with melted butter. Place another 2 sheets of filo on top and brush the top one with butter. Line the dish, letting the excess hang over the side.

Spread the filling in the dish and then fold the overhanging pastry over the top. Butter 2 sheets of filo, place one on top of the other and fold in half. Place over the top of the filling and tuck in the edges. Butter the remaining 3 sheets of pastry and cut roughly into squares. Scrunch these over the top of the pie. Bake for 40 minutes or until crisp and golden.

mini spinach pies

80 ml (3 fl oz/⅓ cup) olive oil
2 onions, finely chopped
2 garlic cloves, chopped
150 g (5 oz) small button mushrooms,
   roughly chopped
200 g (7 oz) English spinach, chopped
½ teaspoon chopped thyme
100 g (4 oz) crumbled feta cheese
750 g (1 lb 10 oz) ready-made shortcrust pastry
milk, to glaze

makes 24

method Heat 2 tablespoons of the oil in a frying pan over medium heat and cook the onion and garlic for 5 minutes, or until soft and lightly coloured. Add the mushrooms and cook for 4 minutes, or until softened. Transfer to a bowl.

Heat 1 tablespoon of the oil in the same pan over medium heat, add half the spinach and cook, stirring well, for 2–3 minutes, until softened. Add to the bowl. Repeat with the remaining oil and spinach. Add the thyme and feta to the bowl and mix. Season well and leave to cool.

Preheat the oven to 200°C (400°F/Gas 6) and grease two 12-hole round-based patty pans or mini muffin tins. Roll out half the pastry between two sheets of baking paper and cut out 24 rounds with a 7.5 cm (3 inch) cutter. Use these to line the patty tins, then add the spinach filling. Roll out the remaining pastry and cut rounds of 7 cm (2¾ inches) to fit the tops of the pies. Press the edges with a fork to seal.

Prick the pie tops once with a fork, brush with milk and bake for 15–20 minutes, or until golden. Serve immediately or leave to cool on a wire rack.

potato and salmon parcels

750 g (1 lb 10 oz) floury potatoes, peeled
40 g (1½ oz) butter
60 ml (2 fl oz/¼ cup) cream
125 g (5 oz/1 cup) grated cheddar cheese
210 g (7 oz) tinned red salmon, skin and
bones removed, flaked
1 tablespoon chopped dill
4 spring onions (scallions), finely chopped
3 sheets puff pastry
1 egg, lightly beaten, to glaze

makes 12

method Cut the potatoes into small pieces and cook in a saucepan of boiling water until tender. Mash with the butter and the cream until there are no lumps. Lightly grease two oven trays.

Add the grated cheese, salmon, dill and spring onion to the potato and mix well. Preheat the oven to 200°C (400°F/Gas 6). Cut each pastry sheet into four squares and divide the salmon mixture among the squares. Lightly brush the edges with the egg. Bring all four corners to the centre to form a point and press together to make a parcel.

Put the parcels on the greased trays and glaze with the egg. Bake for 15–20 minutes, or until the pastry is golden brown.

note *Before removing the pastries from the oven, lift them gently off the tray and check that the bottom of the parcels are cooked through. Take care not to overcook the parcels or they may burst open.*

chicken and corn pies

1 tablespoon olive oil
650 g (1 lb 7 oz) boneless, skinless chicken
   thighs, cut into small pieces
1 tablespoon grated ginger
400 g (14 oz) oyster mushrooms, halved
3 corn cobs, kernels removed
125 ml (4 fl oz/½ cup) chicken stock
2 tablespoons kecap manis (see Note)
2 tablespoons cornflour (cornstarch)
90 g (3 oz/1 bunch) coriander (cilantro),
   leaves chopped
6 sheets shortcrust pastry
milk, to glaze

makes 6

method Grease six 10 cm (4 inch) metal pie tins. Heat the oil in a large frying pan over high heat and add the chicken. Cook for 5 minutes, or until golden. Add the ginger, mushrooms and corn and cook for 5–6 minutes, until the chicken is just cooked through. Add the stock and kecap manis. Mix the cornflour with 2 tablespoons water, then stir into the pan. Boil for 2 minutes before adding the coriander. Cool and then chill for 2 hours.

Preheat the oven to 180°C (350°F/Gas 4). Using a saucer as a guide, cut a 15 cm (6 inch) round from each sheet of shortcrust pastry and line the pie tins. Fill the shells with the cooled filling, then cut out another six rounds large enough to make the lids. Trim away any extra pastry and seal the edges with a fork. Decorate with pastry scraps. Prick a few holes in the top of each pie, brush with a little milk and bake for 35 minutes, until golden.

note *Kecap manis is a thick, sweet soy sauce. If you can't find it, use regular soy sauce mixed with a little soft brown sugar.*

beef and caramelised onion pie

80 ml (3 fl oz/⅓ cup) oil
2 large red onions, thinly sliced
1 teaspoon dark brown sugar
1 kg (2 lb 4 oz) lean rump steak, diced
30 g (1 oz/¼ cup) plain (all-purpose) flour, seasoned
2 garlic cloves, crushed
225 g (8 oz) button mushrooms, sliced
250 ml (9 fl oz/1 cup) beef stock
150 ml (5 fl oz) stout
1 tablespoon tomato paste (concentrated purée)
1 tablespoon worcestershire sauce
1 tablespoon chopped thyme
350 g (12 oz) potatoes, diced
2 carrots, diced
600 g (1 lb 5 oz) ready-made flaky pastry
1 egg, lightly beaten, to glaze

serves 6–8

method Heat 2 tablespoons of the oil in a frying pan over medium heat and cook the onion for 5 minutes, or until light brown. Add the sugar and cook for another 7–8 minutes, or until the onion caramelises. Remove from the pan, set aside and wipe the pan clean.

Toss the beef in the flour and shake off the excess. Heat the remaining oil in the same pan and cook the meat in batches over high heat until browned. Return all the meat to the pan, add the garlic and mushrooms and cook for 2 minutes. Add the beef stock, stout, tomato paste, worcestershire sauce and thyme. Bring to the boil, then reduce the heat and simmer, covered, for 1 hour. Add the diced potato and carrot and simmer for 30 minutes. Remove from the heat and allow to cool.

Preheat the oven to 190°C (375°F/Gas 5). Grease a 1.25 litre (5 cup) pie dish. Pour in the filling and top with the onion. Roll the pastry out between two sheets of baking paper until it is 2.5 cm (1 inch) wider than the pie dish. Cut a 2 cm (¾ inch) strip around the edge of the pastry, brush with water and then place damp side down on the rim of the dish.

Cover with the remaining pastry and press the edges together. Knock up the rim by making small slashes in the edges of the pastry with the back of a knife. Re-roll the trimmings and use them to decorate the pie. Brush with egg and bake for 35 minutes, or until golden.

cottage pie

2 tablespoons olive oil
2 onions, chopped
2 carrots, diced
1 celery stalk, diced
1 kg (2 lb 4 oz) minced (ground) beef
2 tablespoons plain (all-purpose) flour
375 ml (13 fl oz/1½ cups) beef stock
1 tablespoon soy sauce
1 tablespoon worcestershire sauce
2 tablespoons tomato sauce (ketchup)
1 tablespoon tomato paste
   (concentrated purée)
2 bay leaves
2 teaspoons chopped flat-leaf (Italian) parsley

topping

400 g (14 oz) potatoes, peeled and diced
400 g (14 oz) parsnips, peeled and diced
30 g (1 oz) butter
125 ml (4 fl oz/½ cup) milk

serves 6–8

method   Heat the oil in a large frying pan over medium heat. Cook the onion, carrot and celery, stirring occasionally, for 5 minutes, until softened and lightly coloured. Add the beef and cook for 7 minutes, then stir in the flour and cook for 2 minutes. Add the beef stock, soy sauce, worcestershire sauce, tomato sauce, tomato paste and bay leaves and simmer over low heat for 30 minutes, stirring occasionally. Leave to cool. Remove the bay leaves and stir in the parsley.

To make the topping, boil the potato and parsnip in a pan of salted water for 15–20 minutes, or until cooked through. Drain, return to the pan and mash with the butter and enough of the milk to make a firm mash.

Preheat the oven to 180°C (350°F/Gas 4) and lightly grease a 2.5 litre (10 cup) ovenproof dish. Spoon the filling into the dish and spread the potato topping over it. Fluff with a fork. Bake for 40 minutes, or until golden.

salmon filo pie with dill butter

150 g (5 oz/¾ cup) medium-grain white rice
90 g (3 oz) butter, melted
8 sheets filo pastry
500 g (1 lb 2 oz) salmon fillet,
cut into small cubes
2 French shallots (eschallots), finely chopped
1½ tablespoons baby capers
150 g (5 oz/⅔ cup) Greek-style yoghurt
1 egg
1 tablespoon grated lemon zest
3 tablespoons chopped dill
30 g (1 oz/¼ cup) dry breadcrumbs
1 tablespoon sesame seeds
2 teaspoons lemon juice

serves 6–8

method Put the rice in a large saucepan and add enough water to cover it by 2 cm (1 inch). Bring to the boil over medium heat, then reduce the heat to low, cover and cook for 20 minutes, or until all the water has been absorbed and tunnels appear on the surface of the rice. Set aside to cool.

Preheat the oven to 180°C (350°F/Gas 4). Grease a 20 x 30 cm (8 x 12 inch) baking tin with melted butter. Cover the filo pastry with a damp tea towel (dish towel). Mix the salmon with the shallots, capers, rice, yoghurt and egg. Add the lemon zest, 1 tablespoon of the dill and season well.

Layer four sheets of filo pastry in the base of the tin, brushing each one with melted butter and leaving the sides of the pastry hanging over the edge of the tin. Spoon in the salmon filling and pat down well. Fold the pastry over the filling. Top with four sheets of filo, brushing each one with melted butter and sprinkling all but the top layer with a tablespoon of breadcrumbs. Sprinkle the top with sesame seeds.

Score the top of the pie into diamonds without cutting right through the pastry. Bake for 35–40 minutes on the lowest shelf until golden brown. Reheat the remaining butter, add the lemon juice and remaining dill and pour a small amount over each portion of pie.

spinach and feta triangles

1 kg (2 lb 4 oz) English spinach
60 ml (2 fl oz/¼ cup) olive oil
1 onion, chopped
10 spring onions (scallions), sliced
4 tablespoons chopped flat-leaf
  (Italian) parsley
1 tablespoon chopped dill
large pinch of ground nutmeg
35 g (1 oz/⅓ cup) grated parmesan cheese
150 g (5 oz/1 cup) crumbled feta cheese
90 g (3 oz/⅓ cup) ricotta cheese
4 eggs, lightly beaten
40 g (1½ oz) butter, melted
1 tablespoon olive oil, extra
12 sheets filo pastry

makes 8

method Trim any coarse stems from the spinach. Wash the leaves thoroughly, roughly chop and place in a large saucepan with just a little water clinging to the leaves. Cover and cook gently over low heat for 5 minutes, or until the leaves have wilted. Drain well and allow to cool slightly before squeezing tightly to remove the excess water. Chop.

Heat the oil in a frying pan. Add the onion and cook over low heat for 10 minutes, or until it is soft and golden. Add the spring onion and cook for a further 3 minutes. Remove from the heat. Stir in the drained spinach, parsley, dill, nutmeg, cheeses and egg. Season well.

Preheat the oven to 180°C (350°F/Gas 4) and grease two baking trays. Combine the melted butter with the extra oil. Work with three sheets of pastry at a time, keeping the rest covered with a damp tea towel (dish towel). Brush each sheet with butter mixture and lay on top of each other. Cut in half lengthways.

Place 4 tablespoons of the filling on an angle at the end of each strip. Fold the pastry over to enclose the filling and form a triangle. Continue folding over until you reach the end of the pastry. Put on the baking trays and brush with the remaining butter mixture. Bake for 20–25 minutes, or until the pastry is golden brown.

variation *If you are unable to buy English spinach, silverbeet (Swiss chard) can be used instead. Use the same quantity and trim the coarse white stems from the leaves.*

italian easter pie

450 g (1 lb) spinach or silverbeet (Swiss chard),
stalks removed
90 g (3 oz/1 heaped cup) fresh
white breadcrumbs
250 ml (9 fl oz/1 cup) milk
500 g (1 lb 2 oz/2 cups) ricotta cheese
(see Note)
200 g (7 oz/2 cups) grated parmesan cheese
8 eggs
pinch of ground nutmeg
pinch of cayenne pepper
10 small marjoram leaves
150 g (5 oz) butter
20 sheets filo pastry

serves 6–8

method   Bring 500 ml (17 fl oz/2 cups) salted water to the boil in a large saucepan. Add the spinach or silverbeet, cover and cook, stirring occasionally, for 5 minutes, or until wilted. Drain well. When cool enough to handle, wring out all the liquid in a clean tea towel (dish towel). Chop well.

Preheat the oven to 180°C (350°F/Gas 4). Put the breadcrumbs and milk in a large bowl and leave for 5 minutes. Add the ricotta, half the parmesan, 4 eggs, the nutmeg, cayenne, marjoram and chopped spinach. Season and mix.

Melt the butter and lightly brush a 23 cm (9 inch) spring-form tin. Line the base and side with a sheet of filo pastry. Brush with the melted butter and place another filo sheet on top, positioned so that any exposed wall of the tin is covered. Continue in this way, using a total of 10 sheets of filo. Don't worry about the filo forming folds on the tin walls, just push them flat as you brush with the butter.

Spoon the filling into the tin. Make four deep indentations in the surface around the edge of the pie, then break an egg into each. Season and sprinkle with the remaining grated parmesan. Fold over any overhanging pastry. Cover with the remaining filo, buttering each layer.

Bake for 40 minutes, cover the top with foil, then bake for another 20 minutes. Leave to cool in the tin for 20 minutes before serving.

note   *Use ricotta from a wheel as pre-packaged ricotta tends to be too moist.*

steak and kidney pie

750 g (1 lb 10 oz) round steak
4 lamb kidneys
2 tablespoons plain (all-purpose) flour
1 tablespoon oil
1 onion, chopped
30 g (1 oz) butter
1 tablespoon worcestershire sauce
1 tablespoon tomato paste
  (concentrated purée)
125 ml (4 fl oz/½ cup) red wine
250 ml (9 fl oz/1 cup) beef stock
125 g (5 oz) button mushrooms, sliced
½ teaspoon dried thyme
4 tablespoons chopped parsley
375 g (13 oz) ready-made puff pastry
1 egg, lightly beaten, to glaze

serves 6

method Cut the meat into small cubes. Trim the skin from the kidneys. Quarter the kidneys and trim away any fat or sinew. Coat the meat and kidneys with the flour and shake off the excess.

Heat the oil in a pan. Add the onion and cook for 5 minutes, or until soft. Remove with a slotted spoon. Add the butter to the pan. Brown the meat and kidneys in batches and then return all the meat and onion to the pan.

Add the worcestershire sauce, tomato paste, wine, stock, mushrooms, thyme and parsley to the pan. Bring to the boil then simmer, covered, for 1 hour, or until the meat is tender. Season and leave to cool. Spoon the mixture into a 1.5 litre (6 cup) pie dish.

Preheat the oven to 210°C (415°F/ Gas 6–7). Roll out the puff pastry on a lightly floured surface so that it is 5 cm (2 inches) larger than the dish. Cut thin strips from the pastry and press onto the rim, sealing the joins. Place the pastry on top of the pie. Trim the edges and cut steam holes in the top. Decorate with pastry trimmings and brush the top with the egg. Bake for 35–40 minutes, or until golden brown.

chicken and mushroom pithivier

50 g (2 oz) butter
2 bacon slices, sliced
4 spring onions (scallions), chopped
100 g (4 oz) button mushrooms, sliced
1 tablespoon plain (all-purpose) flour
185 ml (6 fl oz/¾ cup) milk
1 tablespoon cream
180 g (6 oz/1 cup) chopped cooked
chicken breast
4 tablespoons chopped parsley
2 sheets puff pastry
1 egg yolk, lightly beaten, to glaze

serves 4

method Melt the butter in a pan. Cook the bacon and spring onion, stirring, for 2–3 minutes. Add the mushrooms and cook, stirring, for 3 minutes. Stir in the flour and cook for 1 minute. Add the milk all at once and stir for 2–3 minutes, or until thickened. Simmer for 1 minute then remove from the heat. Stir in the cream, chicken and parsley. Set aside to cool.

Cut two 23 cm (9 inch) circles from the pastry sheets. Place one circle on a greased baking tray. Pile the filling in the centre, mounding slightly in the middle and leaving a small border. Combine the egg yolk with 1 teaspoon water, and brush the pastry edge.

Using a small pointed knife and starting from the centre of the second pastry circle, mark curved lines at regular intervals. Take care not to cut through the pastry. Place this sheet over the other and stretch it a little to fit evenly. Press the edges together to seal. Using the back of a knife, push up the outside edge at 1 cm (½ inch) intervals. Cover and refrigerate for at least 30 minutes.

Preheat the oven to 210°C (415°F/Gas 6–7). Brush the pie with egg and make a hole in the centre for steam to escape. Bake for 25 minutes, or until golden.

savoury tarts

vegetable tart with salsa verde

215 g (8 oz/1¾ cups) plain (all-purpose) flour
120 g (4 oz) chilled butter, cubed
60 ml (2 fl oz/¼ cup) cream
1–2 tablespoons iced water

salsa verde

1 garlic clove
3 large handfuls flat-leaf (Italian) parsley
80 ml (3 fl oz/⅓ cup) extra virgin olive oil
3 tablespoons chopped dill
1½ tablespoons dijon mustard
1 tablespoon red wine vinegar
1 tablespoon drained baby capers

filling

1 large (250 g/9 oz) waxy potato, cut into
    2 cm (¾ inch) cubes
1 tablespoon olive oil
2 garlic cloves, crushed
1 red capsicum (pepper), cut into cubes
1 red onion, sliced
2 zucchini (courgettes), sliced
2 tablespoons chopped dill
1 tablespoon chopped thyme
1 tablespoon drained baby capers
150 g (5 oz) marinated quartered artichoke
    hearts, drained
30 g (1 oz/⅔ cup) baby English spinach leaves

serves 6

method Sift the flour and ½ teaspoon salt into a large bowl. Rub in the butter with your fingertips until it resembles fine breadcrumbs. Add the cream and most of the water and mix with a knife until it comes together in beads, adding more water if necessary. Gather together on a lightly floured work surface, press into a disc, wrap in plastic wrap and chill for 30 minutes.

Preheat the oven to 200°C (400°F/Gas 6) and grease a 27 cm (10¾ inch) loose-based flan (tart) tin. Roll the dough out between two sheets of baking paper until large enough to line the tin, trimming off the excess. Cover with baking paper, then fill with some baking beads or rice and bake for 15–20 minutes. Remove the paper and beads, reduce the heat to 180°C (350°F/Gas 4) and bake for 20 minutes, or until the pastry is golden.

Mix all the salsa verde ingredients in a food processor until almost smooth.

Boil the potato until just tender. Drain. Heat the oil in a large frying pan and cook the garlic, capsicum and onion for 3 minutes, stirring often. Add the zucchini, dill, thyme and capers and cook for 3 minutes. Reduce the heat, add the potato and artichokes, and heat through. Season to taste.

Spread 60 ml (2 fl oz/¼ cup) of the salsa verde over the pastry base. Spoon the filling into the case and drizzle with half the remaining salsa. Pile the spinach leaves in the centre and drizzle over the last of the salsa verde.

tomato, parmesan and anchovy tart

60 ml (2 fl oz/¼ cup) olive oil
1 onion, finely chopped
2 tablespoons chopped parsley
1 teaspoon dried basil
1 teaspoon sugar
2 x 800 g (1 lb 12 oz) tins tomatoes, drained
2 sheets shortcrust pastry
2 teaspoons chopped anchovy fillets
2 tablespoons grated parmesan cheese
3 eggs, lightly beaten

serves 6–8

method Heat the oil in a frying pan and gently fry the onion for 15 minutes, or until golden. Add the parsley, basil and sugar and cook for 20–30 seconds, stirring constantly. Drain the tomatoes and chop into a pulp. Add to the pan, reduce the heat and simmer for 30 minutes, or until the mixture is dark and quite dry. Cool.

Preheat the oven to 180°C (350°F/Gas 4). Grease a 23 cm (9 inch) shallow fluted loose-based flan (tart) tin. Roll the pastry sheets together, one on top of the other, to 3 mm (¹/₈ inch) thick. Line the tin with the pastry and prick with a fork. Line the pastry with baking paper, fill with baking beads or rice and bake for 10 minutes. Remove the baking paper and beads and bake for 10 minutes, or until dry.

Stir the anchovies, parmesan cheese and eggs through the filling, then spoon into the pastry case and level the surface. Bake for 40 minutes, or until set.

salami, eggplant and artichoke tart

125 g (4½ oz/1 cup) plain (all-purpose) flour
60 g (2 oz) butter, chilled and cubed
1 egg yolk
1–2 tablespoons iced water

filling

2 tablespoons oil
250 g (9 oz) eggplant (aubergine), cubed
110 g (4 oz/½ cup) quartered marinated
    artichokes
125 g (5 oz) piece salami, cubed
1 tablespoon chopped chives
1 tablespoon chopped parsley
1 egg, lightly beaten
60 ml (2 fl oz/¼ cup) cream

serves 4–6

method Put the flour and butter in a food processor and process for 15 seconds, or until crumbly. Add the egg yolk and water and process in short bursts until the mixture just comes together, adding a little more water if necessary. Turn the mixture onto a floured surface and gather together into a ball. Wrap in plastic and refrigerate for at least 20 minutes. Preheat the oven to 200°C (400°F/Gas 6). Grease a shallow 20 cm (8 inch) loose-based flan (tart) tin.

Roll out the pastry on a sheet of baking paper to line the tin and trim off any excess. Refrigerate for 10 minutes. Prick the pastry with a fork and bake for 10 minutes, until lightly browned. Cool.

Heat the oil and toss the eggplant over high heat until it begins to brown and soften; drain on paper towels. Mix the eggplant, artichokes, salami and herbs and press firmly into the pastry case. Pour over the combined egg and cream and bake for 45 minutes, or until browned and set.

fried green tomato tart

4 green tomatoes
1 tablespoon olive oil
20 g (1 oz) butter
1 teaspoon ground cumin
2 garlic cloves, crushed
1 sheet puff pastry
60 g (2 oz/¼ cup) sour cream
1 tablespoon chopped basil
2 tablespoons chopped parsley
60 g (2 oz/½ cup) grated cheddar cheese

serves 6

method Cut the tomatoes into thin slices. Heat the oil and butter in a frying pan and fry the cumin and garlic for 1 minute. Fry the tomatoes in batches for 2–3 minutes, until slightly softened. Drain on paper towels.

Preheat the oven to 200°C (400°F/Gas 6). Cut a 24 cm (9½ inch) round from the puff pastry and place on a greased baking tray. Make a 2 cm (¾ inch) border by scoring gently around the edge. Make small cuts inside the border. Refrigerate for 15 minutes, then bake for 10–15 minutes.

Combine the sour cream, basil and half the parsley. Sprinkle the cheddar cheese over the centre of the pastry. Arrange a layer of tomatoes around the inside edge of the border and then add the rest. Bake for 20 minutes, or until the pastry is golden. Spoon the cream mixture into the middle and sprinkle over the remaining parsley.

cheese and chive soufflé tart

80 g (3 oz) butter
40 g (1½ oz/⅓ cup) plain (all-purpose) flour
250 ml (9 fl oz/1 cup) cream
160 g (6 oz/⅔ cup) sour cream
4 eggs, separated
130 g (5 oz/1 cup) grated gruyère cheese
3 tablespoons chopped chives
¼ teaspoon ground nutmeg
pinch of cayenne pepper
12 sheets filo pastry

serves 6–8

method   Preheat the oven to 190°C (375°F/ Gas 5). Grease a deep 20 cm (8 inch) pie dish or loose-based fluted flan (tart) tin.

Melt half the butter in a saucepan. Sift in the flour and cook, stirring, for 1 minute. Remove from the heat and gradually whisk in the cream and sour cream. Return to the heat and whisk constantly until the mixture boils and thickens. Remove from the heat and whisk in the egg yolks. Then cover the surface with plastic wrap and set aside to allow to cool slightly. Whisk in the cheese, chives, nutmeg and cayenne pepper.

Melt the remaining butter and brush some over each sheet of pastry. Fold each one in half and use to line the flan tin, allowing the edges to overhang.

Beat the egg whites until stiff peaks form, then stir a spoonful into the cheese mixture to loosen it up. Gently fold in the rest of the beaten egg white. Spoon the mixture into the pastry shell and then fold the pastry over the top. Brush the top with the remaining melted butter and bake for 40–45 minutes, or until puffed and golden. Serve immediately.

sweet potato, potato and onion tart

125 g (4½ oz/1 cup) plain (all-purpose) flour
90 g (3 oz) butter, chilled and cubed
1–2 tablespoons iced water

filling

400 g (14 oz) orange sweet potato, peeled
400 g (14 oz) potatoes, peeled
1 onion, thinly sliced
250 ml (9 fl oz/1 cup) cream
2 eggs
1 tablespoon wholegrain mustard

serves 4–6

method Mix the flour and butter in a food processor until the mixture resembles fine breadcrumbs. Add the water and process for 5 seconds to combine. Turn onto a lightly floured surface and gather into a smooth ball.

Roll out the pastry on a sheet of baking paper large enough to fit the base and sides of a 23 cm (9 inch) flan (tart) tin. Trim away the excess and chill for 15 minutes. Preheat the oven to 190°C (375°F/Gas 5).

Cover the pastry with a piece of baking paper, fill with baking beads or rice and bake for 10 minutes. Discard the paper and beads and bake for another 10 minutes. Cool.

Thinly slice the sweet potato and potato. Cook in a steamer for 15 minutes, or until just tender. Drain off any liquid, cover and set aside.

Layer the sweet potato and potato in the pastry shell, in an overlapping pattern, with the onion, gently pushing the layers in to compact them, finishing with onion. Combine the cream, eggs and mustard, season and pour over the tart. Bake for 45 minutes, or until golden.

fresh herb tart

150 g (5½ oz/1¼ cups) plain (all-purpose) flour
100 g (3½ oz) butter, chilled and cubed
1–2 tablespoons iced water
250 g (9 oz/1 cup) light sour cream
125 ml (4 fl oz/½ cup) thick (double/heavy) cream
2 eggs, lightly beaten
1 tablespoon chopped thyme
2 tablespoons chopped parsley
1 tablespoon chopped oregano

serves 4–6

method   Put the flour and butter in a food processor. Process for 15 seconds, or until the mixture resembles fine breadcrumbs. Add most of the water and process in short bursts until the mixture just comes together, adding a little more water if needed. Turn onto a floured surface and gather the pastry into a ball. Cover with plastic wrap and chill for at least 20 minutes.

Roll out the pastry on a sheet of baking paper to line a 35 x 10 cm (14 x 4 inch) loose-based flan (tart) tin. Trim away the excess pastry. Refrigerate for 10 minutes. Preheat the oven to 200°C (400°F/Gas 6).

Cover the pastry shell with baking paper and fill evenly with baking beads or rice. Place on a baking tray and bake for 20 minutes. Remove the paper and beads and reduce the oven temperature to 180°C (350°F/Gas 4). Cook for 15–20 minutes, or until golden and dry. Cool.

Whisk together the sour cream, thickened cream and eggs until smooth. Then stir in the herbs and season. Place the pastry shell on a baking tray and pour in the filling. Bake for 25–30 minutes, or until set. Allow to stand for 15 minutes before serving and cutting.

roasted tomato and garlic tart

4 roma (plum) tomatoes, halved
1 tablespoon olive oil
1 teaspoon balsamic vinegar
1 teaspoon salt
5–10 garlic cloves, unpeeled
2 sheets puff pastry
1 egg, lightly beaten
10 bocconcini (fresh baby mozzarella cheese), halved

serves 4

method Preheat the oven to 200°C (400°F/Gas 6). Put the tomatoes, cut side up, on a baking tray and drizzle with the olive oil, balsamic vinegar and salt. Bake for 20 minutes. Add the garlic and bake for a further 15 minutes. Cool and squeeze or peel the garlic from its skin.

Grease a 35 x 10 cm (14 x 4 inch) loose-based fluted flan (tart) tin. Lay a sheet of pastry over each end of the tin, so that they overlap in the middle and around the edges. Seal the sheets together with egg and trim the edges. Cover with baking paper and fill with baking beads or rice and bake for 15 minutes. Remove the paper and beads and bake for 10 minutes.

Place the roasted tomatoes along the centre of the tart and fill the gaps with the garlic and bocconcini. Bake for a further 10 minutes and serve.

french shallot tatin

750 g (1 lb 10 oz) French shallots (eschallots)
50 g (2 oz) butter
2 tablespoons olive oil
60 g (2 oz/⅓ cup) soft brown sugar
60 ml (2 fl oz/¼ cup) balsamic vinegar
125 g (4½ oz/1 cup) plain (all-purpose) flour
60 g (2 oz) butter, chilled and cubed
2 teaspoons wholegrain mustard
1 egg yolk
1–2 tablespoons iced water

serves 4–6

method   Peel the shallots, leaving the bases intact and tips exposed. Heat the butter and olive oil in a large saucepan and cook the shallots over low heat for 15 minutes, then remove. Add the sugar, vinegar and 60 ml (2 fl oz/¼ cup) water and stir to dissolve the sugar. Return the shallots to the pan and simmer over low heat for 15–20 minutes, turning occasionally.

Preheat the oven to 200°C (400°F/Gas 6). Process the flour and butter in a food processor until crumbly. Add the mustard, egg yolk and most of the water. Process in short bursts until the mixture just comes together, adding more water if necessary. Turn onto a floured surface and gather into a ball. Wrap in plastic and refrigerate for 20 minutes.

Grease a shallow 20 cm (8 inch) round sandwich tin. Tightly pack the shallots into the tin and pour over syrup from the pan. Roll out the pastry on a sheet of baking paper to a circle, 1 cm (½ inch) larger than the tin. Lift the pastry into the tin and lightly push it down so it is slightly moulded over the shallots. Bake for 20–25 minutes, or until golden brown. Cool for 5 minutes on a wire rack. Place a plate over the tin and turn the tart out.

hint   *Put the unpeeled shallots in boiling water for 30 seconds to make them easier to peel.*

feta tart with beetroot

110 g (4 oz/¾ cup) plain wholemeal
(whole-wheat) flour
90 g (3 oz/¾ cup) plain (all-purpose) flour
125 g (4½ oz) butter, chilled and cubed
1 egg yolk
1–2 tablespoons iced water
300 g (11 oz) ricotta cheese
300 g (11 oz) crumbled feta cheese
3 eggs, lightly beaten
300 g (11 oz) baby beetroot (beets),
with short stalks attached
1 tablespoon walnut or olive oil
1 tablespoon red wine vinegar
30 g (1 oz/¼ cup) chopped pecans
2 tablespoons coriander (cilantro) leaves

serves 6

method Place the flours, butter and a pinch of salt in a food processor and process for 15 seconds, until crumbly. Add the egg yolk and most of the water and process in short bursts until the mixture just comes together, adding more water if needed. Turn onto a floured surface and gather into a ball. Wrap in plastic and chill for 15 minutes. Preheat the oven to 180°C (350°F/Gas 4).

Mix the cheeses together with a fork. Add the eggs and mix well. Grease a 23 cm (9 inch) loose-based flan (tart) tin. Roll out the pastry on a floured surface to line the tin, press it into the sides and trim off any excess pastry. Cover with baking paper, fill with baking beads or rice and bake for 10 minutes. Remove the paper and beads and bake for a further 10 minutes.

Spoon the filling into the base and bake for 30 minutes, or until the filling is firm and puffed (the filling will flatten slightly when removed from the oven).

Boil or steam the beetroots until tender, then peel and cut in half. Drizzle with the combined oil and vinegar, and season well. Serve the beetroot, chopped pecans and coriander with the tart.

spicy chicken tarts

2 large onions, finely chopped
400 g (14 oz) eggplant (aubergine), cubed
2 garlic cloves, crushed
2 x 410 g (14 oz) tins chopped tomatoes
1 tablespoon tomato paste
  (concentrated purée)
3 teaspoons soft brown sugar
1 tablespoon red wine vinegar
3 tablespoons chopped parsley
4 sheets shortcrust pastry
2 teaspoons ground cumin seeds
2 teaspoons ground coriander
1 teaspoon paprika
400 g (14 oz) boneless, skinless
  chicken breasts
olive oil, for cooking
sour cream, to serve
coriander (cilantro) leaves, to serve

makes 8

method Fry the onion in a little oil until golden. Add the eggplant and garlic and cook for a few minutes. Stir in the tomato, tomato paste, sugar and vinegar. Bring to the boil, reduce the heat, cover and simmer for 20 minutes. Uncover and simmer for 10 minutes, or until thickened. Add the parsley and season. Preheat the oven to 190°C (375°F/Gas 5).

Grease eight 7.5 cm (3 inch) pie tins, line with the pastry and decorate the edges with a spoon. Prick the bases with a fork. Bake for 15 minutes, or until golden.

Mix the cumin seeds, coriander and paprika on baking paper. Coat the chicken breasts in the spices. Heat some oil in a frying pan and cook the chicken for 10 minutes, turning regularly, or until brown and cooked through. Slice the fillets diagonally.

Fill the pie shells with the eggplant mixture and decorate with the sliced chicken, sour cream and coriander leaves.

mushroom and ricotta filo tart

60 g (2 oz) butter
270 g (10 oz) field mushrooms, sliced
2 garlic cloves, crushed
1 tablespoon Marsala
1 teaspoon thyme leaves
½ teaspoon chopped rosemary leaves
pinch of grated nutmeg
5 sheets filo pastry
75 g (2 oz) butter, melted
200 g (7 oz) ricotta cheese
2 eggs, lightly beaten
125 g (5 oz/½ cup) sour cream
1 tablespoon chopped flat-leaf (Italian) parsley

serves 6

method   Preheat the oven to 180°C (350°F/Gas 4). Melt the butter in a frying pan over high heat and cook the mushrooms for a few minutes, until they begin to soften. Add the garlic, cook for another minute, then stir in the Marsala, thyme, rosemary and nutmeg. Remove the mushrooms from the pan and drain off any liquid.

Work with 1 sheet of filo pastry at a time, keeping the rest covered with a damp tea towel (dish towel) to stop them drying out. Brush the sheets with melted butter and fold in half. Place on top of each other to line a shallow 23 cm (9 inch) loose-based flan (tart) tin, allowing the pastry to hang over the rim.

Beat the ricotta, eggs and sour cream together and season to taste. Spoon half the mixture into the tin, then layer the mushrooms. Top with the rest of the ricotta mixture. Loosely fold the overhanging pastry over the filling. Bake for 35 minutes, or until firm. Sprinkle with the parsley.

caramelised onion, rocket and blue cheese tarts

250 g (9 oz/2 cups) plain (all-purpose) flour
125 g (4½ oz) butter, chilled and cubed
30 g (1 oz/¼ cup) grated parmesan cheese
1 egg, lightly beaten
60 ml (2 fl oz/¼ cup) iced water

filling

2 tablespoons olive oil
3 onions, thinly sliced
100 g (4 oz) baby rocket (arugula) leaves
100 g (4 oz) blue cheese, crumbled
3 eggs, lightly beaten
60 ml (2 fl oz/¼ cup) cream
60 g (2 oz/½ cup) grated parmesan cheese
pinch of grated nutmeg

makes 6

method   In a large bowl, rub the butter into the sifted flour until it resembles fine breadcrumbs. Stir in the parmesan. Make a well in the centre, add the egg and iced water and mix with a flat-bladed knife, using a cutting action, until the mixture forms beads. Turn the pastry onto a lightly floured work surface, press into a disc, wrap in plastic and chill for 30 minutes.

Preheat the oven to 200°C (400°F/Gas 6). Divide the pastry into six portions and roll out each portion between two sheets of baking paper to fit an 8 cm (3¼ inch) fluted loose-based flan (tart) tin. Trim off the excess.

Line the pastry shells with baking paper large enough to cover the base and side of each tin and cover with baking beads or rice. Bake for 10 minutes, then remove the paper and beads and bake for a further 10 minutes, or until the base is dry and golden. Cool slightly. Reduce the oven to 180°C (350°F/Gas 4).

Heat the oil in a large frying pan, add the onion and cook over medium heat for 20 minutes, or until the onion is caramelised. Add the rocket and stir until wilted. Remove from the pan and cool.

Divide the mixture between the tart bases and sprinkle with the blue cheese. Whisk together the eggs, cream, parmesan and nutmeg and pour evenly over each of the tarts. Place on a baking tray and bake for 20–30 minutes. Serve hot or cold.

potato and zucchini tart

185 g (6½ oz/1½ cups) plain (all-purpose) flour
125 g (4½ oz) butter, chilled and cubed
1 egg yolk
1–2 tablespoons iced water

filling

450 g (1 lb) floury potatoes, peeled
and roughly chopped
40 g (1½ oz/⅓ cup) plain (all-purpose) flour
125 g (5 oz) jarlsberg cheese, grated
80 ml (3 fl oz/⅓ cup) cream
2 eggs, separated
2 small zucchini (courgettes),
thinly sliced lengthways
4 thyme sprigs, to garnish

serves 6–8

method Put the flour in a bowl with ½ teaspoon salt. Rub in the butter with your fingertips, until the mixture resembles fine breadcrumbs. Add the egg yolk and most of the water and mix with a knife to form a rough dough, adding more water if necessary. Turn onto a lightly floured surface and work into a smooth ball, then wrap in plastic wrap and refrigerate for 15 minutes. Preheat the oven to 190°C (375°F/Gas 5).

Grease a 25 cm (10 inch) loose-based flan (tart) tin. On a lightly floured surface, roll out the dough large enough to fit the tin, and trim off the excess pastry. Cover with baking paper and fill with baking beads or rice. Bake for 10 minutes and discard the paper and beads. Bake for another 5–10 minutes.

To make the filling, boil the potato until tender. Drain, cool for 5 minutes and mash. Mix in the flour and cheese, then stir in 170 ml (5½ fl oz/⅔ cup) water and, when loosely incorporated, add the cream. Whisk until smooth, then add the egg yolks and combine well. Season with salt and white pepper. Beat the egg whites in a small bowl until stiff peaks form, fold into the mashed potato mixture and gently pour into the pie crust.

Arrange the zucchini over the pie in a decorative pattern. Decorate with the thyme sprigs and bake for 35–45 minutes, until set and golden brown. Serve hot or at room temperature.

italian summer tart

185 g (6½ oz/1½ cups) plain (all-purpose) flour
90 g (3 oz) butter, chilled and cubed
1 egg yolk
2–3 tablespoons iced water

filling

1 tablespoon olive oil
2 small red onions, sliced
1 tablespoon balsamic vinegar
1 teaspoon soft brown sugar
1 tablespoon thyme leaves
170 g (6 oz) jar marinated quartered artichokes,
  drained
4 slices prosciutto, cut into strips
12 black olives

serves 4–6

method Process the flour and butter in a food processor for 15 seconds, or until the mixture resembles fine breadcrumbs. Add the egg yolk and iced water. Process in short bursts until the mixture just comes together, adding a little extra water if necessary. Turn onto a lightly floured work surface and gather together into a ball. Cover with plastic wrap and refrigerate for at least 30 minutes.

Roll the pastry between two sheets of baking paper until large enough to fit a 35 x 10 cm (14 x 4 inch) loose-based flan tin. Press it into the sides and trim off the excess. Cover and refrigerate for 20 minutes.

Preheat the oven to 190°C (375°F/Gas 5).Cover the pastry shell with baking paper and fill evenly with baking beads or rice. Bake for 15 minutes, then remove the paper and beads and bake for a further 15 minutes, or until the pastry is golden and dry. Cool on a wire rack.

To make the filling, heat the oil in a saucepan, add the onion slices and cook, stirring occasionally, for 15 minutes. Add the vinegar and sugar and cook for a further 15 minutes. Remove from the heat, stir through the thyme leaves and set aside to cool.

Spread the onion mixture evenly over the pastry shell. Arrange the quartered artichoke pieces on top, then fill the spaces between the artichokes with rolled-up pieces of prosciutto and the black olives. Serve the tart at room temperature.

pesto and anchovy tart

pesto

3 large handfuls basil leaves
2 garlic cloves
50 g (2 oz/½ cup) grated parmesan cheese
80 g (3 oz/½ cup) pine nuts, toasted
60 ml (2 fl oz/¼ cup) olive oil

375 g (13 oz) ready-made puff pastry
1 egg yolk, lightly beaten
45 g (1½ oz) tin anchovies, drained
50 g (2 oz/⅓ cup) grated mozzarella cheese
35 g (1 oz/⅓ cup) grated parmesan cheese

serves 6

method To make the pesto, put the basil, garlic, parmesan and pine nuts in a food processor and chop finely. With the motor running, slowly add the oil and process until well combined.

Preheat the oven to 200°C (400°F/Gas 6). Roll the pastry into a rectangle 18 x 35 cm (7 x 14 inches), and 5 mm (¼ inch) thick. Cut a 2 cm (¾ inch) strip all the way round the edge of the pastry. Combine the egg yolk with 1 teaspoon water and brush around the edge of the pastry. Trim the pastry strips to fit around the rectangle and then attach them to form a crust. Place on a lightly floured baking tray and, using the tip of a sharp knife, make small cuts all over the base. Bake for 15 minutes. Press the centre of the pastry down with the back of a spoon and bake for a further 5 minutes, or until lightly golden. Allow to cool.

Spread the pesto evenly over the pastry base. Cut the anchovies into strips and arrange over the pesto. Sprinkle the grated mozzarella and parmesan over the top and bake for 10 minutes, or until golden.

tomato and thyme tart

250 g (9 oz/2 cups) plain (all-purpose) flour
125 g (4½ oz) butter, chilled and cubed
125 g (4½ oz) cream cheese, chopped
1 tablespoon thyme leaves

filling

40 g (1½ oz/½ cup) fresh breadcrumbs
30 g (1 oz/¼ cup) grated parmesan cheese
2 tablespoons lemon thyme leaves
6 roma (plum) tomatoes, sliced
3 spring onions (scallions), sliced
1 egg yolk, beaten with 1 teaspoon of water,
   to glaze

serves 6–8

method   Mix the flour, butter, cream cheese and thyme in a food processor. Add 2 tablespoons of water and process in short bursts until the mixture just comes together, adding more water if needed. Turn onto a floured surface and gather together into a ball. Press into a large triangle, cover with plastic wrap and chill for 15 minutes.

Preheat the oven to 210°C (415°F/Gas 6–7). Place the pastry on a greased baking tray and prick all over with a fork. Place the breadcrumbs, most of the parmesan and 1 tablespoon of the lemon thyme on the pastry, leaving an 8 cm (3¼ inch) border all around the edge. Overlap the tomatoes and scatter some of the spring onions on top, maintaining the border. Add freshly ground black pepper, the remaining spring onions, parmesan cheese and lemon thyme.

Fold the pastry border over the filling, pleating as you go, and press to seal. Brush with the egg glaze and bake for 10 minutes. Reduce the oven temperature to 180°C (350°F/Gas 4) and cook for a further 15–20 minutes, or until golden.

mediterranean ricotta tarts

30 g (1 oz/⅓ cup) dry breadcrumbs
2 tablespoons olive oil
1 garlic clove, crushed
½ red capsicum (pepper), quartered and
cut into thin strips
1 zucchini (courgette), cut into thin strips
3 slices prosciutto, cut into thin strips
375 g (13 oz/1½ cups) firm ricotta cheese
(see Note)
40 g (1½ oz/⅓ cup) grated cheddar cheese
30 g (1 oz/⅓ cup) grated parmesan cheese
2 tablespoons shredded basil
4 black olives, pitted and sliced

makes 6

method Preheat the oven to 180°C (350°F Gas 4). Lightly grease six 10 cm (4 inch) fluted (tart) flan tins. Lightly sprinkle 1 teaspoon breadcrumbs over the base and side of each tin.

Heat half the oil in a frying pan, add the garlic, capsicum and zucchini and cook, stirring, over medium heat for 5 minutes, or until the vegetables are soft. Remove from the heat and add the prosciutto. Season to taste.

Place the ricotta in a large bowl and add the other cheeses and the remaining breadcrumbs. Season. Press the mixture into the tins and smooth the surface. Bake for 20 minutes, or until the tarts are slightly puffed and golden. Cool completely (the tarts will deflate on cooling) and remove from the tins, but do not refrigerate.

Sprinkle the bases with basil and divide the vegetable mixture between them. Top with the olives then drizzle with the remaining oil.

note *Use firm ricotta or very well-drained ricotta, or the tarts will be difficult to remove from the tins.*

vol-au-vents

250 g (9 oz) ready-made puff pastry
1 egg, lightly beaten
40 g (1½ oz) butter
2 spring onions (scallions), finely chopped
2 tablespoons plain (all-purpose) flour
375 ml (13 fl oz/1½ cups) milk
your choice of filling (see Note)

makes 4

method Preheat the oven to 220°C (425°F/Gas 7) and line a baking tray with baking paper. Roll out the pastry to a 20 cm (8 inch) square. Cut four circles of pastry with a 10 cm (4 inch) cutter. Place the rounds onto the tray and score 6 cm (2½ inch) circles into the centre of the rounds with a cutter, taking care not to cut right through the pastry. Refrigerate for 15 minutes.

Use a floured knife blade to knock up the sides of each pastry round by indenting every 1 cm (½ inch) around the rim. Brush with the egg, carefully avoiding the edge as any glaze spilt on the side will stop the pastry from rising. Bake for 20 minutes, until golden brown and crisp. Cool on a wire rack. Remove the centre from each pastry circle and pull out and discard any partially cooked pastry from the centre. Return to the oven for 2 minutes to dry out if the centre is undercooked.

Melt the butter in a saucepan, add the spring onion and stir over low heat for 2 minutes, or until soft. Add the flour and stir for 2 minutes, or until lightly golden. Gradually add the milk, stirring until smooth. Stir constantly over medium heat for 4 minutes, or until the mixture boils and thickens. Season well. Remove from the heat and stir in your choice of filling before spooning into the cases to serve.

note *Add 350 g (12 oz) of any of the following to the sauce: sliced, cooked mushrooms; peeled, cooked prawns (shrimp); chopped, cooked chicken breast; poached, flaked salmon; dressed crabmeat; oysters; steamed asparagus spears.*

100 EASY RECIPES PIES AND TARTS

roasted tomato and zucchini tartlets

3 roma (plum) tomatoes, halved lengthways
1 teaspoon balsamic vinegar
1 teaspoon olive oil
3 small zucchini (courgettes), sliced
3 sheets ready-rolled puff pastry
1 egg yolk, beaten, to glaze
12 small black olives
24 capers, rinsed and drained

pistachio mint pesto

75 g (3 oz/½ cup) unsalted shelled
pistachio nuts
3 large handfuls mint leaves
2 garlic cloves, crushed
80 ml (3 fl oz/⅓ cup) olive oil
50 g (2 oz/½ cup) grated parmesan cheese

makes 6

method   Preheat the oven to 150°C (300°F/Gas 2). Place the tomatoes, cut side up, on a baking tray. Roast for 30 minutes, brush with the combined vinegar and oil and roast for a further 30 minutes. Increase the oven temperature to 210°C (415°F/Gas 6–7).

To make the pesto, place the pistachios, mint and garlic in a food processor and process for 15 seconds. With the motor running, slowly pour in the olive oil. Add the parmesan and process briefly.

Preheat the grill (broiler) and line with foil. Place the zucchini in a single layer on the foil and brush with the remaining balsamic vinegar and oil. Grill for about 5 minutes, turning once.

Roll out the pastry to 25 x 40 cm (10 x 16 inches) and cut out six 12 cm (4 inch) circles. Put the circles on a greased baking tray and brush with the egg yolk. Spread a tablespoon of pesto on each, leaving a 2 cm (¾ inch) border. Divide the zucchini among the pastries, top with tomato halves and bake for 15 minutes, or until golden. Top with olives, capers and black pepper.

quiches

blue cheese and onion quiche

2 tablespoons olive oil
1 kg (2 lb 4 oz) red onions, very thinly sliced
1 teaspoon soft brown sugar
250 g (9 oz/2 cups) plain (all-purpose) flour
100 g (3½ oz) butter, chilled and cubed
1–2 tablespoons iced water
185 ml (6 fl oz/¾ cup) cream
3 eggs
100 g (4 oz) blue cheese, crumbled
1 teaspoon chopped thyme

serves 8

method   Heat the oil in a pan over low heat and cook the onion and sugar, stirring regularly, for 45 minutes, or until the onion is lightly golden.

Process the flour and butter in a food processor for 15 seconds, or until crumbly. Add most of the iced water and process in short bursts until the mixture just comes together, adding more water if necessary. Turn the pastry out onto a floured surface and gather into a ball. Wrap in plastic wrap and refrigerate for 10 minutes.

Preheat the oven to 180°C (350°F/Gas 4). Roll out the pastry on a lightly floured surface to fit a greased 22 cm (8½ inch) loose-based flan (tart) tin. Trim away the excess pastry. Refrigerate for 10 minutes.

Line the pastry with baking paper and spread with a layer of baking beads or rice. Place on a baking tray and bake for 10 minutes. Remove the paper and beads, then bake for another 10 minutes, or until lightly golden and dry. Cool, then gently spread the onion in the pastry shell.

Whisk together the cream, eggs, blue cheese, thyme and some freshly ground black pepper to taste. Pour into the base and bake for 35 minutes, or until firm.

fresh salmon and dill quiche

200 g (7 oz/1⅔ cups) plain (all-purpose) flour
125 g (4½ oz) butter, chilled and cubed
1 teaspoon icing (confectioners') sugar
1–2 tablespoons iced water

filling

2 eggs
1 egg yolk
250 ml (9 fl oz/1 cup) cream
1 teaspoon finely grated lemon zest
2 tablespoons finely chopped
spring onions (scallions)
450 g (1 lb) fresh salmon fillet, bones and skin
removed, cut into bite-sized chunks
1 tablespoon chopped dill

serves 4–6

method Process the flour, butter and icing sugar in a food processor for about 15 seconds until crumbly. Add most of the water. Process in short bursts until the mixture just comes together. Add a little more water if needed. Turn out onto a floured surface and gather into a ball. Wrap in plastic and refrigerate for 15 minutes.

Roll the pastry between two sheets of baking paper until large enough to fit a 23 cm (9 inch) loose-based flan (tart) tin. Trim away the excess pastry and refrigerate for 15 minutes. Preheat the oven to 180°C (350°F/Gas 4).

To make the filling, lightly beat the eggs and egg yolk. Add the cream, lemon zest and spring onion and season well. Cover and set aside.

Prick the base of the pastry shell with a fork. Cover with baking paper and a layer of baking beads or rice. Bake for 15 minutes, or until lightly golden. Remove the paper and beads and arrange the salmon over the base. Scatter with the dill and then pour in the egg mixture. Bake for 40 minutes, or until the salmon is cooked and the filling has set. Serve warm or cool.

quiche lorraine

185 g (6½ oz/1½ cups) plain (all-purpose) flour
90 g (3¼ oz) butter, chilled and cubed
1 egg yolk
2–3 tablespoons iced water

filling

20 g (1 oz) butter
1 onion, chopped
4 bacon slices, cut into thin strips
2 tablespoons chopped chives
2 eggs
185 ml (6 fl oz/¾ cup) cream
60 ml (2 fl oz/¼ cup) milk
100 g (4 oz) Swiss cheese, grated

serves 4–6

method Mix the flour and butter in a food processor for 15 seconds, or until crumbly. Add the egg yolk and water. Process in short bursts until the mixture just comes together. Add a little more water if needed. Turn out onto a floured surface and gather together into a ball. Wrap the dough in plastic and refrigerate for at least 15 minutes.

Roll the pastry between two sheets of baking paper until large enough to line a shallow 25 cm (10 inch) loose-based flan (tart) tin. Press well into the side of the tin and trim off any excess pastry. Refrigerate the pastry-lined tin for 20 minutes. Preheat the oven to 190°C (375°F/Gas 5).

Cover the pastry shell with baking paper, spread with a layer of baking beads or rice and bake for 15 minutes. Remove the paper and beads and bake the pastry shell for 10 minutes, or until the pastry is golden and dry. Reduce the oven temperature to 180°C (350°F/Gas 4).

To make the filling, heat the butter in a frying pan. Add the onion and bacon and cook for 10 minutes, stirring frequently, until the onion is soft and the bacon is cooked. Stir in the chives and leave to cool.

Beat together the eggs, cream and milk. Season with freshly ground black pepper. Spread the filling evenly into the pastry shell. Pour the egg mixture over the top and sprinkle with the cheese. Bake for 30 minutes, or until the filling is set and golden.

spicy sweet potato quiche

250 g (9 oz/2 cups) plain (all-purpose) flour
125 g (4½ oz) butter, chilled and cubed
1 egg yolk
2–3 tablespoons iced water

filling

30 g (1 oz) butter
1 onion, sliced
1 garlic clove, crushed
2 teaspoons black mustard seeds
2 teaspoons ground cumin
1 teaspoon soft brown sugar
450 g (1 lb) orange sweet potato, chopped
2 eggs, lightly beaten
60 ml (2 fl oz/¼ cup) milk
60 ml (2 fl oz/¼ cup) cream
2 tablespoons chopped parsley
2 tablespoons chopped chives

serves 6

method Process the flour and butter in a food processor for 15 seconds, or until crumbly. Add the egg yolk and most of the water. Process in short bursts until the mixture comes together, adding more water if necessary. Turn out onto a floured surface and gather into a ball. Roll the pastry between two sheets of baking paper until large enough to line a shallow 23 cm (9 inch) loose-based fluted flan (tart) tin. Trim away the excess pastry. Refrigerate for 20 minutes.

For the filling, heat the butter in a large saucepan and cook the onion and garlic for 5 minutes, or until golden. Add the mustard seeds, cumin and sugar and stir for 1 minute. Add the sweet potato and cook for 10 minutes over low heat until it has softened slightly. Stir gently, or the sweet potato will break up.

Preheat the oven to 180°C (350°F/Gas 4). Line the pastry shell with baking paper and fill with baking beads or rice. Bake for 15 minutes, then remove the paper and beads and bake for a further 15 minutes.

Put the sweet potato mixture into the pastry shell. Mix together the egg, milk, cream, parsley and chives and pour over the sweet potato. Bake for 50 minutes, or until set.

eggplant and sun-dried capsicum quiches

185 g (6½ oz/1½ cups) plain (all-purpose) flour
125 g (4½ oz) butter, chilled and cubed
1 egg yolk
1 tablespoon iced water

filling

100 g (4 oz) slender eggplants (aubergines),
   thinly sliced
30 g (1 oz) butter
4 spring onions (scallions), finely chopped
1–2 garlic cloves, crushed
½ small red capsicum (pepper), finely chopped
40 g (1½ oz/¼ cup) sun-dried capsicums
   (peppers), drained and chopped
2 eggs, lightly beaten
185 ml (6 fl oz/¾ cup) cream

makes 6

method   Process the flour and butter for about 15 seconds until crumbly. Add the egg yolk and water. Process in short bursts until the mixture comes together. Add a little extra water if needed. Turn out onto a floured surface and gather into a ball. Wrap in plastic and refrigerate for at least 30 minutes.

Brush the eggplant slices with olive oil and grill (broil) until browned. Heat the butter in a small pan and cook the spring onion, garlic and capsicum for 5 minutes, stirring frequently, until soft. Add the sun-dried capsicum and leave to cool. Combine egg and cream in a bowl and season well.

Grease six 8 cm (3 inch) fluted tart tins. Roll out the pastry thinly to line the tins, and trim. Cover and refrigerate for 15 minutes. Preheat the oven to 190°C (375°F/Gas 5). Cover the pastry shells with baking paper and a layer of baking beads or rice. Bake for 10 minutes. Remove the paper and beads and bake for 10 minutes.

Divide the filling among the pastry shells, top with the eggplant and pour over the cream and egg mixture. Bake for 25–30 minutes, or until set.

low-fat roast vegetable quiche

1 small potato, peeled
200 g (7 oz) pumpkin (winter squash), peeled
100 g (4 oz) orange sweet potato, peeled
1 large parsnip, peeled
½ red capsicum (pepper)
1 onion, cut into wedges
3 garlic cloves, halved
1 teaspoon olive oil
200 g (7 oz/1⅔ cups) plain (all-purpose) flour
55 g (2 oz) butter, chilled and cubed
60 g (2 oz/¼ cup) ricotta cheese
250 ml (9 fl oz/1 cup) skim milk
3 eggs, lightly beaten
30 g (1 oz/¼ cup) grated reduced-fat cheddar cheese

serves 6–8

method Preheat the oven to 180°C (350°F/Gas 4). Lightly grease a 23 cm (9 inch) loose-based flan (tart) tin. Cut the potato, pumpkin, sweet potato, parsnip and capsicum into bite-sized chunks, place in a baking dish with the onion and garlic and drizzle with the oil. Season and bake for 1 hour, or until tender. Leave to cool.

Process the flour, butter and ricotta cheese in a food processor until crumbly, then gradually add 80 ml (3 fl oz/⅓ cup) of the milk, or enough to form a soft dough. Turn out onto a lightly floured surface and gather into a smooth ball. Cover and refrigerate for 15 minutes.

Roll out the pastry on a lightly floured surface and then ease into the tin, bringing it gently up the side. Trim the edge and refrigerate for another 10 minutes. Increase the oven to 200°C (400°F/Gas 6). Cover the pastry with baking paper and spread with a layer of baking beads or rice. Bake for 10 minutes, then remove the paper and beads and bake for 10 minutes, or until golden brown and dry.

Combine the remaining milk, the egg and cheese. Place the vegetables in the pastry base and pour the mixture over the top. Reduce the oven to 180°C (350°F/Gas 4) and bake for 1 hour 10 minutes, or until set in the centre. Leave for 5 minutes before removing from the tin to serve.

seafood quiche

2 sheets shortcrust pastry
30 g (1 oz) butter
300 g (11 oz) mixed raw seafood
90 g (3 oz/¾ cup) grated cheddar cheese
3 eggs
1 tablespoon plain (all-purpose) flour
125 ml (4 fl oz/½ cup) cream
125 ml (4 fl oz/½ cup) milk
1 small fennel bulb, finely sliced
1 tablespoon grated parmesan cheese

serves 4–6

method   Grease a 23 cm (9 inch) loose-based fluted flan (tart) tin. Lay the pastry sheets so they slightly overlap and roll out until large enough to fit the tin. Press well into the sides and trim off the excess pastry. Refrigerate for 20 minutes. Preheat the oven to 190°C (375°F/Gas 5).

Cover the pastry shell with baking paper and spread with a layer of baking beads or rice. Bake for 15 minutes. Remove the paper and beads and bake for 10 minutes, until golden. Cool on a wire rack.

Heat the butter in a pan and cook the seafood for 2–3 minutes. Leave to cool. Arrange in the pastry shell and sprinkle with the cheddar cheese.

In a bowl, beat the eggs together and whisk in the flour, ¼ teaspoon salt, ½ teaspoon freshly ground black pepper, cream and milk. Pour over the seafood filling. Sprinkle the fennel and parmesan cheese over the top. Bake for 30–35 minutes. Leave to cool slightly before serving.

mushroom quiche with parsley pastry

310 g (11 oz/2½ cups) plain (all-purpose) flour
30 g (1 oz/½ cup) chopped parsley
180 g (6 oz) butter, chilled and cubed
2 egg yolks
80 ml (2½ fl oz/⅓ cup) iced water

filling

30 g (1 oz) butter
1 red onion, chopped
175 g (6 oz) button mushrooms, sliced
1 teaspoon lemon juice
4 tablespoons chopped parsley
4 tablespoons chopped chives
2 eggs, lightly beaten
170 ml (6 fl oz/⅔ cup) cream

serves 4–6

method Process the flour, parsley and butter in a food processor for 15 seconds, or until crumbly. Add the egg yolk and most of the iced water. Process in short bursts until the mixture comes together, adding a little more water if needed. Turn out onto a floured surface and gather into a ball. Cover with plastic wrap and refrigerate for at least 30 minutes.

Roll out the pastry between two sheets of baking paper until large enough to line a 35 x 10 cm (14 x 4 inch) loose-based flan (tart) tin. Trim away the excess pastry. Refrigerate for 20 minutes. Preheat the oven to 190°C (375°F/Gas 5).

Line the pastry with baking paper and spread with a layer of baking beads or rice. Bake for 15 minutes. Remove the paper and beads and bake for another 10 minutes, or until the pastry is dry. Reduce the oven to 180°C (350°F/Gas 4).

Melt the butter in a pan and cook the onion for 2–3 minutes until soft. Add the mushrooms and cook, stirring, for 2–3 minutes until soft. Stir in the lemon juice and herbs. In a bowl, mix the egg and cream together and season. Spread the mushroom mixture into the pastry shell and pour over the egg and cream. Bake for 25–30 minutes, or until the filling has set.

green peppercorn and gruyère quiches

2 sheets puff pastry
100 g (4 oz) gruyère cheese, diced
½ small celery stalk, finely chopped
1 teaspoon chopped thyme
2 teaspoons green peppercorns, chopped
1 egg, lightly beaten
60 ml (2 fl oz/¼ cup) cream

makes 4

method Grease four deep 8 cm (3¼ inch) loose-based flan (tart) tins. Use a 14 cm (5½ inch) cutter to cut two rounds from each sheet of pastry. Lift the pastry into the tins and press into the sides. Trim the excess pastry with a sharp knife or by rolling a rolling pin across the top of the tins. Prick the bases with a fork. Refrigerate for at least 15 minutes.

Preheat the oven to 220°C (425°F/Gas 7). Bake the pastry shells for about 12 minutes, or until they are browned and puffed. Remove from the oven and, as the pastry is cooling, gently press down the bases if they have puffed too high—this will make room for the filling.

Mix together the cheese, celery, thyme and peppercorns and spoon into the pastry cases. Combine the egg and cream and pour over the top. Bake for 25–30 minutes, or until the filling is puffed and set.

caramelised onion quiche

185 g (6½ oz/1½ cups) plain (all-purpose) flour
125 g (4½ oz) butter, chilled and cubed
1 egg yolk
1–2 tablespoons iced water

filling

800 g (1 lb 12 oz) onions, thinly sliced
75 g (3 oz) butter
1 tablespoon soft brown sugar
185 g (7 oz/¾ cup) sour cream
2 eggs
40 g (1½ oz) prosciutto, cut into strips
40 g (1½ oz/⅓ cup) grated cheddar cheese
2 teaspoons thyme leaves

serves 6

method Process the flour and butter in a food processor until crumbly. Add the egg yolk and most of the water. Process in short bursts until the mixture comes together, adding more water if needed. Turn out onto a floured surface and gather into a ball. Wrap in plastic and refrigerate for 20 minutes.

Blanch the onion in boiling water for 2 minutes, then drain. Melt the butter in a saucepan over low heat and cook the onion for 25 minutes, or until soft. Stir in the brown sugar and cook for 15 minutes, stirring occasionally.

Preheat the oven to 200°C (400°F/Gas 6). Grease a 23 cm (9 inch) loose-based flan (tart) tin. Roll out the pastry until large enough to fit the tin and trim off the excess. Cover with baking paper and spread with baking beads or rice. Bake for 15 minutes. Remove the paper and beads and bake for 5 minutes.

Lightly beat the sour cream and eggs together. Add the prosciutto, cheese and thyme. Stir in the onion and pour the mixture into the pastry shell. Bake for 40 minutes, or until set. If the pastry starts to over-brown, cover with foil.

asparagus and parmesan quiche

185 g (6½ oz/1½ cups) plain (all-purpose) flour
125 g (4½ oz) butter, chilled and cubed
1 egg yolk
2 tablespoons iced water

filling

50 g (2 oz/½ cup) grated parmesan cheese
30 g (1 oz) butter
1 small red onion, chopped
2 spring onions (scallions), chopped
1 tablespoon chopped dill
1 tablespoon chopped chives
1 egg, lightly beaten
60 g (2 oz/¼ cup) sour cream
60 ml (2 fl oz/¼ cup) cream
400 g (13 oz) tinned asparagus spears, drained

serves 4–6

method Process the flour and butter in a food processor for about 15 seconds, or until crumbly. Add the egg yolk and most of the iced water. Process in short bursts until the mixture just comes together. Add a little more water if needed. Turn onto a floured surface and gather into a ball. Wrap in plastic wrap and refrigerate for 30 minutes.

Roll out the pastry between two sheets of baking paper to fit a 35 x 10 cm (14 x 4 inch) loose-based flan (tart) tin. Trim away the excess pastry and refrigerate for 20 minutes. Preheat the oven to 190°C (375°F/Gas 5).

Line the pastry with baking paper and fill with a layer of baking beads or rice. Bake for 15 minutes. Remove the paper and beads and bake for another 10 minutes, or until the pastry is dry and golden. Cool slightly, then sprinkle with half the parmesan cheese. Reduce the oven to 180°C (350°F/Gas 4).

Melt the butter in a saucepan and cook the onion and spring onion for 2–3 minutes until soft. Stir in the herbs and cool. In a bowl, whisk together the egg, sour cream, cream and remaining parmesan cheese and season well.

Spread the onion mixture over the pastry. Lay the asparagus spears over the top and pour over the egg mixture. Bake for 25–30 minutes, or until set.

feta, basil and olive quiche

150 g (5½ oz/1¼ cups) flour, sifted
90 g (3 oz) butter, melted and cooled
60 ml (2 fl oz/¼ cup) milk

filling

200 g (7 oz) feta cheese, cubed
1 handful basil, shredded
30 g (1 oz/¼ cup) sliced black olives
3 eggs, lightly beaten
80 ml (3 fl oz/⅓ cup) milk
90 g (3 oz/⅓ cup) sour cream

serves 6

method Grease a deep 23 cm (9 inch) loose-based flan (tart) tin. Place the flour in a large bowl and make a well in the centre. Add the butter and milk and stir until the mixture comes together to form a dough. Turn out onto a floured surface and gather into a ball. Refrigerate for 5 minutes. Roll out the pastry and place in the tin, press it well into the sides and trim the edge. Chill for 20 minutes. Preheat the oven to 200°C (400°F/ Gas 6).

To make the filling, spread the feta over the base of the pastry and top with the basil and olives. Whisk the eggs, milk and sour cream until smooth, then pour into the pastry shell. Bake for 15 minutes, then reduce the oven temperature to 180°C (350°F/Gas 4) and cook for a further 25 minutes, or until the filling is firmly set. Serve at room temperature.

artichoke and provolone quiches

250 g (9 oz/2 cups) plain (all-purpose) flour
125 g (4½ oz) butter, chilled and cubed
1 egg yolk
60 ml (2 fl oz/¼ cup) iced water

filling

1 small eggplant (aubergine), sliced
olive oil, for brushing
6 eggs, lightly beaten
3 teaspoons wholegrain mustard
150 g (5 oz) provolone cheese, grated
200 g (7 oz) marinated artichokes, sliced
125 g (5 oz/1 cup) semi-dried (sun-blushed)
  tomatoes

makes 6

method Process the flour and butter in a food processor for 15 seconds, or until crumbly. Add the egg yolk and most of the water. Process in short bursts until the mixture comes together. Add a little more water if needed. Turn onto a floured surface and gather into a ball. Wrap in plastic and chill for at least 30 minutes.

Preheat the oven to 190°C (375°F/Gas 5) and grease six 11 cm (4¼ inch) oval or round pie tins.

To make the filling, brush the eggplant with olive oil and grill (broil) until golden. Mix together the egg, mustard and cheese.

Roll out the pastry to line the tins. Trim away the excess pastry and decorate the edges. Place one eggplant slice in each tin and top with the artichokes and tomatoes. Pour the egg mixture over the top and bake for 25 minutes, or until golden.

mustard chicken and asparagus quiche

250 g (9 oz/2 cups) plain (all-purpose) flour
100 g (3½ oz) butter, chilled and cubed
1 egg yolk
60 ml (2 fl oz/¼ cup) iced water

filling

150 g (5 oz) asparagus, chopped
25 g (1 oz) butter
1 onion, chopped
60 g (2 oz/¼ cup) wholegrain mustard
200 g (7 oz) soft cream cheese
125 ml (4 fl oz/½ cup) cream
3 eggs, lightly beaten
200 g (7 oz) cooked chicken, chopped
½ teaspoon black pepper

serves 6

method Process the flour and butter in a food processor until crumbly. Add the egg yolk and most of the water. Process in short bursts until the mixture comes together. Add a little more water if needed. Turn onto a floured surface and gather into a ball. Wrap in plastic and refrigerate for 30 minutes. Grease a deep 20 cm (8 inch) loose-based flan (tart) tin.

Preheat the oven to 200°C (400°F/Gas 6). Roll out the pastry and line the tin. Trim off any excess. Place the tin on a baking tray and chill for 10 minutes. Line the pastry with baking paper and fill with baking beads or rice. Bake for 10 minutes. Remove the paper and beads and bake for another 10 minutes, or until the pastry is lightly browned and dry. Cool. Reduce the oven to 180°C (350°F/Gas 4).

To make the filling, boil or steam the asparagus until tender. Drain and pat dry with paper towel. Heat the butter in a pan and cook the onion until translucent. Remove from the heat and add the wholegrain mustard and cream cheese. Stir until the cheese has melted, then leave to cool. Add the cream, eggs, chicken and asparagus and mix well.

Spoon the filling into the pastry shell and sprinkle with the black pepper. Bake for 50 minutes–1 hour, or until puffed and set. Cover the surface with foil if it browns before the quiche is set. Cool for at least 15 minutes before cutting.

leek and ham quiche with polenta pastry

125 g (4½ oz/1 cup) plain (all-purpose) flour
75 g (2½ oz/½ cup) polenta
90 g (3¼ oz) butter, chilled and cubed
90 g (3¼ oz) cream cheese, chilled and cubed

filling

50 g (2 oz) butter
2 leeks, white part only, thinly sliced
3 eggs, lightly beaten
375 ml (13 fl oz/1½ cups) cream
½ teaspoon ground nutmeg
80 g (3 oz) ham, chopped
75 g (3 oz) Swiss cheese, grated

serves 6

method Process the flour and polenta briefly to mix together. Add the butter and cream cheese and process for about 15 seconds, until the mixture comes together. Add 1–2 tablespoons of iced water if needed. Turn out onto a floured surface and gather into a ball. Wrap in plastic wrap and refrigerate for 30 minutes.

Heat the butter in a pan and add the leeks. Cover and cook for 10–15 minutes, stirring often, until soft but not brown. Cool. Mix together the egg, cream and nutmeg and season with pepper.

Grease a shallow 21 x 28 cm (8¼ x 11¼ inch) loose-based flan (tart) tin with melted butter. Roll the pastry between baking paper until large enough to fit the tin and trim off any excess pastry. Refrigerate for 20 minutes. Preheat the oven to 190°C (375°F/Gas 5).

Cover the pastry shell with baking paper and baking beads or rice. Bake for 15 minutes. Remove the paper and beads and bake for 15 minutes, until the pastry is golden and dry. Reduce the oven to 180°C (350°F/Gas 4).

Spread the leek over the pastry shell and sprinkle with the ham and cheese. Pour in the cream mixture. Bake for 30 minutes, or until golden and set.

smoked salmon and caper quiche

185 g (6½ oz/1½ cups) plain (all-purpose) flour
90 g (3 oz) butter, chilled and cubed
2 teaspoons cracked black pepper
1 egg yolk
2 tablespoons iced water

filling

1 tablespoon olive oil
1 small leek, white part only, chopped
½ teaspoon sugar
200 g (7 oz) sliced smoked salmon
50 g (2 oz/⅓ cup) frozen peas
2 tablespoons baby capers
75 g (3 oz) cream cheese
2 eggs
2 teaspoons dijon mustard
185 ml (6 fl oz/¾ cup) cream

serves 6–8

method Process the flour and butter in a food processor for 15 seconds, or until crumbly. Add the pepper, egg yolk and most of the water. Process in short bursts until the mixture comes together, adding more water if necessary. Turn onto a floured surface and gather into a ball. Cover with plastic wrap and chill for 30 minutes.

Preheat the oven to 200°C (400°F/Gas 6). Grease a 17 cm (6½ inch) deep loose-based fluted flan (tart) tin. Lay the pastry in the tin, place on a baking tray and refrigerate for 10 minutes. Prick the base with a fork and bake for 12 minutes.

To make the filling, heat the oil in a pan and cook the leek and sugar over low heat for 15 minutes. Cool, then spoon into the pastry. Scrunch up the salmon slices and lay around the edge. Put the peas and capers in the centre.

Process the cream cheese, eggs and dijon mustard in a food processor until smooth. Add the cream and pour into the pastry shell. Bake for 40 minutes, or until set.

blue cheese and parsnip quiche

125 g (4½ oz/1 cup) plain (all-purpose) flour
150 g (5½ oz/1 cup) wholemeal
   (whole-wheat) flour
100 g (3½ oz) butter, chilled and cubed
1 egg yolk
60 ml (2 fl oz/¼ cup) iced water

filling

2 teaspoons oil
1 small onion, chopped
1 carrot, cut into small cubes
1 parsnip, cut into small cubes
1 teaspoon cumin seeds
1 tablespoon chopped coriander
   (cilantro) leaves
100 g (4 oz) mild blue cheese
1 egg, lightly beaten
90 ml (3 fl oz/⅓ cup) cream

serves 4–6

method Process the flours and butter in a food processor until crumbly. Add the egg yolk and iced water. Process in short bursts until the mixture comes together. Add more water if needed. Turn out and gather into a ball. Wrap in plastic and refrigerate for 15 minutes.

Preheat the oven to 200°C (400°F/Gas 6) and heat a baking tray. Grease a deep 19 cm (7½ inch) loose-based fluted flan (tart) tin. Roll out the pastry between two sheets of baking paper. Line the tin and trim the excess. Prick the base with a fork and refrigerate for 10 minutes. Place on the heated tray and bake for 12 minutes, until the pastry is just browned and dry. Leave to cool.

Heat the oil in a pan and cook the onion, carrot, parsnip and cumin seeds, stirring, until the onion is translucent. Add the coriander and season well. Remove from heat and cool slightly.

Crumble the cheese into the pastry shell and spoon in the filling. Mix together the egg and cream and pour over the filling. Sprinkle with fresh pepper. Bake for 45 minutes, until set.

fresh herb quiche

185 g (6½ oz/1½ cups) plain (all-purpose) flour
3 tablespoons chopped parsley
125 g (4½ oz) butter, chilled and cubed
1 egg yolk
1 tablespoon iced water

filling

30 g (1 oz) butter
1 small leek, white part only, thinly sliced
1–2 garlic cloves, crushed
4 spring onions (scallions), chopped
3 tablespoons chopped parsley
2 tablespoons chopped chives
2 tablespoons chopped dill
2 tablespoons oregano leaves
3 eggs
250 ml (9 fl oz/1 cup) cream
60 ml (2 fl oz/¼ cup) milk
125 g (5 oz/1 cup) grated cheddar cheese

serves 4–6

method Process the flour, parsley and butter in a food processor for 15 seconds, or until crumbly. Add the egg yolk and most of the water. Process in short bursts until the mixture comes together. Add a little extra water if needed. Turn onto a floured surface and gather into a ball. Wrap in plastic wrap and refrigerate for 30 minutes.

Preheat the oven to 190°C (375°F/Gas 5) and grease a 24 cm (9½ inch) loose-based flan (tart) tin. Roll out the pastry, line the tin and trim off any excess. Chill the lined tin for 20 minutes. Cover the pastry with baking paper and spread with a layer of baking beads or rice. Bake for 15 minutes. Remove the paper and beads and bake for a further 10 minutes. Reduce the oven to 180°C (350°F/ Gas 4).

Heat the butter in a saucepan and cook the leek, garlic and spring onion for 10 minutes, stirring often. Add the herbs and let cool.

In a bowl, beat the eggs, cream and milk and season with freshly ground black pepper. Spread the leek and herb mixture in the pastry base. Pour over the egg mixture and sprinkle with the cheese. Bake for 25–30 minutes, or until golden.

tomato and thyme quiche

185 g (6½ oz/1½ cups) plain (all-purpose) flour
125 g (4½ oz) butter, chilled and cubed
1 egg yolk
2–3 tablespoons iced water

filling

425 g (15 oz) tin tomatoes
4 eggs
300 g (11 oz) sour cream
25 g (1 oz/¼ cup) grated parmesan cheese
2 spring onions (scallions), finely chopped
1–2 tablespoons chopped thyme

serves 8

method   Preheat the oven to 210°C (415°F/Gas 6–7). Sift the flour into a bowl and rub in the butter until the mixture resembles fine breadcrumbs. Add the combined egg yolk and most of the iced water and mix to a soft dough, adding more water if necessary. Turn onto a lightly floured surface and gather into a ball. Wrap in plastic and refrigerate for 30 minutes.

Roll out the pastry to line a shallow 23 cm (9 inch) flan (tart) tin. Trim off the excess. Line the pastry with baking paper and spread with a layer of baking beads or rice. Bake for 10 minutes, then discard the paper and beads and cook for a further 5 minutes, or until golden.

Drain the tomatoes and halve lengthways. Drain, cut side down, on paper towels. Beat together the eggs and sour cream and stir in the cheese and spring onion. Pour the filling into the pastry shell. Arrange the tomatoes, cut side down, over the filling. Sprinkle with thyme and black pepper. Reduce the oven to 180°C (350°F/Gas 4) and bake for 30 minutes, or until the filling is set and golden.

roasted pumpkin and spinach quiche

500 g (1 lb 2 oz) butternut pumpkin (squash)
1 red onion, cut into small wedges
2 tablespoons olive oil
1 garlic clove, crushed
1 teaspoon salt
4 eggs
125 ml (4 fl oz/½ cup) cream
125 ml (4 fl oz/½ cup) milk
1 tablespoon chopped parsley
1 tablespoon chopped coriander
(cilantro) leaves
1 teaspoon wholegrain mustard
6 sheets filo pastry
50 g (2 oz) English spinach, blanched
1 tablespoon grated parmesan cheese

serves 6

method Preheat the oven to 190°C (375°F/Gas 5). Cut the pumpkin into 1 cm (½ inch) slices, leaving the skin on. Place the pumpkin, onion, 1 tablespoon of the oil, garlic and salt in a baking dish. Roast for 1 hour, or until lightly golden and cooked.

Whisk together the eggs, cream, milk, parsley, coriander and mustard. Season with salt and freshly ground black pepper.

Grease a 23 cm (9 inch) loose-based fluted flan (tart) tin. Brush each sheet of filo pastry with oil and then line the tin with the six sheets. Fold the sides down, tucking them into the tin to form a crust.

Heat a baking tray in the oven for 10 minutes. Place the tart tin on the tray and arrange the vegetables over the base. Pour the egg mixture over the vegetables and sprinkle with the parmesan cheese. Bake for 35–40 minutes, or until the filling is golden brown and set.

sweet pies
and tarts

peach pie

500 g (1 lb 2 oz) ready-made sweet
  shortcrust pastry
2 x 825 g (1 lb 13 oz) tins peach slices, drained
125 g (5 oz/½ cup) caster (superfine) sugar
30 g (1 oz/¼ cup) cornflour (cornstarch)
¼ teaspoon natural almond extract (essence)
20 g (1 oz) unsalted butter, chopped
1 tablespoon milk
1 egg, lightly beaten
1 tablespoon caster (superfine) sugar,
  extra, to sprinkle

serves 6–8

method   Roll out two-thirds of the dough between two sheets of baking paper until large enough to line an 18 cm (7 inch) pie tin, pressing it firmly into the side and trimming away the excess. Refrigerate for 20 minutes.

Preheat the oven to 200°C (400°F/Gas 6). Line the pastry with baking paper and spread with a layer of baking beads or rice. Bake for 10 minutes, then remove the paper and beads and return to the oven for 5 minutes, or until the base is dry and lightly golden. Allow to cool.

Mix the peaches, caster sugar, cornflour and almond extract and spoon into the pastry shell. Dot with butter and moisten the edge with milk.

Roll out the remaining dough to a 25 cm (10 inch) square. Using a fluted pastry cutter, cut the pastry into ten strips, each 2.5 cm (1 inch) wide. Lay the strips in a lattice pattern over the filling. Press firmly on the edges and trim. Brush the lattice with egg and sprinkle with the extra sugar. Bake for 10 minutes, reduce the oven to 180°C (350°F/Gas 4) and bake for another 30 minutes, or until the top is golden.

key lime pie

125 g (5 oz) sweet wheatmeal biscuits
90 g (3 oz) butter, melted
4 egg yolks
400 g (14 oz) tin condensed milk
125 ml (4 fl oz/½ cup) lime juice
2 teaspoons finely grated lime zest
250 ml (9 fl oz/1 cup) cream, to serve

serves 8

method Finely crush the biscuits in a food processor for 30 seconds. Transfer to a bowl, add the butter and mix thoroughly. Press the mixture into a 23 cm (9 inch) pie dish and refrigerate until firm. Preheat the oven to 180°C (350°F/Gas 4).

Beat the egg yolks, condensed milk, lime juice and zest with electric beaters for 1 minute. Pour into the crust and smooth the surface. Bake for 20–25 minutes, or until set. Cool in the tin.

Refrigerate the pie for 2 hours or until well chilled. Serve with cream.

pear and almond flan

150 g (5½ oz/1¼ cups) plain (all-purpose) flour
90 g (3 oz) butter, chilled and cubed
60 g (2 oz/¼ cup) caster (superfine) sugar
2 egg yolks
1 tablespoon iced water

filling

165 g (6 oz) unsalted butter, softened
160 g (6 oz/⅔ cup) caster (superfine) sugar
3 eggs
230 g (8 oz/2¼ cups) ground almonds
1½ tablespoons plain (all-purpose) flour
2 ripe pears

serves 8

method Grease a shallow 24 cm (9½ inch) loose-based flan (tart) tin. Place the flour, butter and sugar in a food processor and process until the mixture resembles breadcrumbs. Add the egg yolks and water and mix until the dough just comes together. Turn out onto a lightly floured surface and gather into a ball. Wrap in plastic wrap and refrigerate for 30 minutes. Preheat the oven to 180°C (350°F/Gas 4).

Roll the pastry between baking paper until large enough to line the tin, trimming any excess. Sparsely prick the base with a fork. Line with baking paper and a layer of baking beads or rice and bake for 10 minutes. Remove the paper and beads and bake for another 10 minutes.

Mix the butter and sugar with electric beaters for 30 seconds (do not cream the mixture). Add the eggs one at a time, beating after each addition. Fold in the ground almonds and flour and spread smoothly over the cooled pastry base.

Peel and halve the pears lengthways and remove the cores. Cut them crossways into 3 mm (⅛ inch) slices. Separate the slices slightly, then place each half on top of the tart to form a cross. Bake the flan for 50 minutes, or until the filling has set (the middle may still be slightly soft). Cool in the tin and refrigerate for at least 2 hours before serving.

low-fat fruit tarts

125 g (4½ oz/1 cup) plain (all-purpose) flour
30 g (1 oz/¼ cup) custard powder
30 g (1 oz/¼ cup) icing (confectioners') sugar
40 g (1½ oz) unsalted butter
2 tablespoons skim milk
2 x 125 g (5 oz) tubs low-fat fromage frais
100 g (4 oz) ricotta cheese
fresh fruit, such as strawberry halves,
blueberries and kiwi fruit slices
3–4 tablespoons redcurrant jelly

makes 6

method Lightly grease six 7 cm (2³/4 inch) shallow loose-based flan (tart) tins. Process the flour, custard powder, icing sugar and butter in a food processor until the mixture forms fine crumbs, then add enough skim milk to form a soft dough. Gather the dough together into a ball, wrap in plastic wrap and refrigerate for 30 minutes. Preheat the oven to 200°C (400°F/Gas 6).

Divide the dough into six portions and roll out to fit the tins. Cover with baking paper and spread with a layer of baking beads or rice. Bake for 10 minutes, remove the paper and beads and bake for another 10 minutes, or until golden. Allow to cool before removing from the tins.

Mix the fromage frais and ricotta until smooth. Spread over the pastry bases and top with the fruit. Heat the redcurrant jelly until liquid in a small saucepan and brush over the fruit.

apple and pecan filo pie

60 g (2 oz/½ cup) pecans
50 g (2 oz) butter
55 g (2 oz/¼ cup) caster (superfine) sugar
1 teaspoon finely grated lemon zest
1 egg, lightly beaten
2 tablespoons plain (all-purpose) flour
3 green apples
10 sheets filo pastry
40 g (1½ oz) butter, melted
icing (confectioners') sugar, to dust

serves 8

method   Preheat the oven to 180°C (350°F/Gas 4). Lightly grease a 35 x 11 cm (14 x 4¼ inch) tin. Spread the pecans in a single layer on an oven tray and bake for 5 minutes to lightly toast. Leave to cool, then chop finely.

Beat the butter, sugar, lemon zest and egg with electric beaters until creamy. Stir in the flour and nuts.

Peel, core and thinly slice the apples. On a flat surface, layer 10 sheets of pastry, brushing each sheet with melted butter before laying the next sheet on top. Fit the layered pastry loosely into the prepared tin. Spread the nut mixture evenly over the pastry base and lay the apple slices on top.

Fold the overhanging pastry over the filling and brush with melted butter. Trim one side of the pastry lengthways and crumple it over the top of the tart. Bake for 45 minutes, or until brown and crisp. Before serving, dust with icing sugar. Serve hot or cold.

storage   *This tart is best eaten on the day it is made.*

variation   *Thinly sliced pears can be used instead of apples. Walnuts can replace the pecans. Toasting the nuts improves their flavour and makes them a little more crunchy.*

pumpkin pie

150 g (5½ oz/1¼ cups) plain (all-purpose) flour
100 g (3½ oz) unsalted butter, chilled
and cubed
2 teaspoons caster (superfine) sugar
80 ml (3 fl oz/⅓ cup) iced water

filling

750 g (1 lb 10 oz) butternut pumpkin (squash),
peeled and cubed
2 eggs, lightly beaten
185 g (7 oz/1 cup) soft brown sugar
80 ml (3 fl oz/⅓ cup) cream
1 tablespoon sweet sherry or brandy
½ teaspoon ground ginger
½ teaspoon ground nutmeg
1 teaspoon ground cinnamon

serves 6–8

method Sift the flour into a large bowl and rub in the butter with your fingertips until the mixture resembles fine breadcrumbs. Add the caster sugar. Make a well in the centre, add almost all the water and mix with a flat-bladed knife, using a cutting action, until the mixture comes together in beads, adding more water if needed. Gather the dough together and lift onto a lightly floured work surface. Press into a disc. Wrap in plastic and refrigerate for 20 minutes.

Roll out the pastry between two sheets of baking paper until large enough to line an 18 cm (7 inch) pie dish. Line the dish with pastry, trim away the excess and use it to decorate the rim. Cover with plastic wrap and refrigerate for 20 minutes.

Preheat the oven to 180°C (350°F/Gas 4).Cook the pumpkin in boiling water until tender. Drain, mash, push through a sieve and leave to cool.

Line the pastry shell with baking paper and spread with a layer of baking beads or rice. Bake the pastry for 10 minutes, then remove the paper and beads and bake for 10 minutes, or until lightly golden. Set aside to cool.

Whisk the eggs and sugar together in a large bowl. Add the cooled pumpkin, cream, sherry and the spices and stir thoroughly. Pour into the pastry shell, smooth the surface and decorate the rim with leftover pastry. Bake for 1 hour, or until set. If the pastry over-browns, cover the edges with foil. Cool before serving.

chocolate-almond tarts

125 g (4½ oz/1 cup) plain (all-purpose) flour
60 g (2 oz) unsalted butter, chilled and cubed
1 tablespoon icing (confectioners') sugar
1 tablespoon lemon juice

filling

1 egg
90 g (3 oz/⅓ cup) caster (superfine) sugar
2 tablespoons cocoa powder
90 g (3 oz/½ cup) ground almonds
60 ml (2 fl oz/¼ cup) cream
80 g (3 oz/¼ cup) apricot jam
18 blanched almonds
icing (confectioners') sugar, to serve

makes 18

method   Preheat the oven to 180°C (350°F/Gas 4). Lightly grease two 12-cup shallow patty pans or mini muffin tins. Mix the flour, butter and icing sugar in a food processor for 10 seconds, or until fine and crumbly. Add the juice and process until the dough forms a ball.

Roll out the dough between two sheets of baking paper to 6 mm (¼ inch) thick. Cut rounds with a 7 cm (2¾ inch) fluted cutter to line the tins and refrigerate for 20 minutes.

Beat the egg and sugar with electric beaters until thick and pale. Sift the cocoa over the top. Using a flat-bladed knife, stir in the ground almonds and cream.

Place a dab of jam in the centre of each pastry base. Spoon the almond filling over the jam and place an almond in the centre of each one. Bake for 15 minutes, or until puffed and set on top. Leave in the tins for 5 minutes, then cool on a wire rack. Sprinkle with icing sugar to serve.

berry ricotta cream tartlets

185 g (6½ oz/1½ cups) plain (all-purpose) flour
90 g (3 oz/½ cup) ground almonds
40 g (1½ oz/⅓ cup) icing (confectioners') sugar
125 g (4½ oz) unsalted butter,
chilled and cubed
1 egg, lightly beaten

filling

200 g (7 oz) ricotta cheese
1 teaspoon natural vanilla extract
2 eggs
160 g (6 oz/⅔ cup) caster (superfine) sugar
125 ml (4 fl oz/½ cup) cream
60 g (2 oz/½ cup) raspberries
80 g (3 oz/½ cup) blueberries
icing (confectioners') sugar, to dust

serves 6

method Sift the flour into a large bowl, then add the ground almonds and icing sugar. Rub in the butter with your fingertips until it resembles fine breadcrumbs. Make a well in the centre, add the egg and mix it in with a flat-bladed knife, using a cutting action, until the mixture comes together in beads. Turn onto a lightly floured work surface and gather into a ball. Wrap in plastic wrap and refrigerate for 30 minutes.

Grease six 8 cm (3¼ inch) deep loose-based flan (tart) tins. Roll out the pastry between two sheets of baking paper to fit the base and side of the tins, trimming away the excess. Prick the bases with a fork, then refrigerate for 30 minutes. Preheat the oven to 180°C (350°F/Gas 4).

Line the pastry bases with baking paper and cover with baking beads or rice. Bake for 8–10 minutes, then remove the paper and beads. Mix the ricotta, vanilla, eggs, sugar and cream in a food processor until smooth. Divide the berries among the tarts and pour over the filling. Bake for 25–30 minutes, or until just set—the top should be soft but not too wobbly. Cool. Dust with icing sugar to serve.

chocolate and peanut butter pie

200 g (7 oz) chocolate biscuits with cream centre, crushed
60 g (2 oz) unsalted butter, melted
250 g (9 oz/1 cup) cream cheese
90 g (3 oz/¾ cup) icing (confectioners') sugar, sifted
125 g (5 oz/½ cup) smooth peanut butter
1 teaspoon natural vanilla extract
300 ml (11 fl oz) cream, whipped
60 ml (2 fl oz/¼ cup) cream, extra
3 teaspoons unsalted butter, extra
100 g (4 oz) dark chocolate, grated
honey-roasted chopped nuts, to garnish

serves 10–12

method Mix the biscuit crumbs with the melted butter and press the mixture into a deep 18 cm (7 inch) pie dish. Refrigerate for 15 minutes.

Beat the cream cheese and icing sugar with electric beaters until smooth. Add the peanut butter and vanilla extract and beat together well. Stir in a little of the whipped cream until the mixture is smooth, then very gently fold in the remaining whipped cream. Pour two-thirds of the filling into the pie shell and smooth the top. Refrigerate the pie and the remaining filling for 2 hours, or until firm.

Put the extra cream and butter in a small saucepan and stir over medium heat until the butter is melted and the cream just comes to a simmer. Remove from the heat and add the grated chocolate. Stir until smooth and silky. Cool to room temperature, then pour over the top of the pie, smoothing if necessary with a spatula dipped in hot water. Refrigerate for 2 hours, or until the topping is firm. Remove the extra filling from the fridge about 30 minutes before you serve.

Fill a piping (icing) bag with the softened filling and pipe rosettes around the edge of the pie. Scatter the nuts around the outer edge. Serve in thin wedges as this pie is rich.

bramble pie

125 g (4½ oz/1 cup) self-raising flour
125 g (4½ oz/1 cup) plain (all-purpose) flour
125 g (4½ oz) unsalted butter, chilled
and cubed
2 tablespoons caster (superfine) sugar
1 egg, lightly beaten
3–4 tablespoons milk

filling

2 tablespoons cornflour (cornstarch)
2–4 tablespoons caster (superfine) sugar,
to taste
1 teaspoon grated orange zest
1 tablespoon orange juice
600 g (1 lb 5 oz) brambles (see Note)
1 egg yolk, mixed with 1 teaspoon water

serves 4–6

method Mix the flours, butter and sugar in a food processor for 30 seconds or until the mixture is fine and crumbly. Add the egg and almost all the milk; process for another 15 seconds or until the mixture comes together, adding more milk if needed. Turn onto a lightly floured surface and gather into a ball. Refrigerate for 30 minutes.

Put the cornflour, sugar, orange zest and juice in a saucepan and mix well. Add half the brambles and stir over low heat for 5 minutes until the mixture boils and thickens. Cool, then add the remaining brambles. Pour into a 750 ml (26 fl oz/3 cup) pie dish.

Preheat the oven to 180°C (350°F/ Gas 4). Divide the dough in half and roll out one half large enough to cover the dish. Trim away the excess. Roll out the other half and use cutters of various sizes to cut out enough hearts to cover the top. Brush the pie top with egg glaze. Bake for 35 minutes or until the top is golden brown.

note *Brambles include any creeping stem berries, such as boysenberries, blackberries, loganberries and youngberries. Use one variety or a combination.*

little lemon tarts

250 g (9 oz/2 cups) plain (all-purpose) flour
125 g (4½ oz) unsalted butter, chilled
  and cubed
2 teaspoons caster (superfine) sugar
1 teaspoon finely grated lemon zest
1 egg yolk
2–3 tablespoons iced water

filling

125 g (5 oz/½ cup) cream cheese, softened
125 g (5 oz/½ cup) caster (superfine) sugar
2 egg yolks
2 tablespoons lemon juice
125 ml (4 fl oz/½ cup sweetened condensed
  milk
icing (confectioners') sugar, for dusting

makes 24

method Preheat the oven to 180°C (350°F/Gas 4) and lightly oil two 12-hole patty pans or mini muffin tins.

Sift the flour into a bowl. Rub in the butter until the mixture resembles fine breadcrumbs. Add the sugar, lemon zest, egg yolk and water and mix with a flat-bladed knife, using a cutting action, until the mixture forms beads. Turn out onto a lightly floured surface and gently gather into a smooth ball. Wrap in plastic wrap and refrigerate for 10 minutes.

Beat the cream cheese, sugar and egg yolks until smooth and thickened. Add the lemon juice and condensed milk and beat together well.

Roll out the dough between two sheets of baking paper to 3 mm (1/8 inch) thick. Cut into rounds with a 7 cm (2¾ inch) fluted cutter and line the patty pans. Lightly prick each base several times with a fork and bake for 10 minutes, or until just starting to turn golden. Spoon 2 teaspoons of filling into each case and bake for another 8–10 minutes, or until the filling has set. Cool slightly before removing from the tins. Dust with the icing sugar to serve.

tarte tatin

100 g (4 oz) unsalted butter
185 g (7 oz/¾ cup) sugar
6 large pink lady or fuji apples, peeled, cored
and quartered (see Note)
1 sheet puff pastry

serves 6

method Preheat the oven to 220°C (425°F/Gas 7). Lightly grease a 23 cm (9 inch) shallow cake tin. Melt the butter in a frying pan, add the sugar and cook, stirring, over medium heat for 4–5 minutes, or until the sugar starts to caramelise and turn brown. Continue to cook, stirring, until the caramel turns golden brown.

Add the apple to the pan and cook over low heat for 20–25 minutes, or until it starts to turn golden brown. Carefully turn the apple over and cook the other side until evenly coloured. If a lot of liquid comes out of the apple, increase the heat until it has evaporated—the caramel should be sticky rather than runny. Remove from the heat. Using tongs, arrange the hot apple in circles in the tin and pour the sauce over the top.

Place the pastry over the apple quarters, tucking the edge down firmly with the end of a spoon. Bake for 30–35 minutes, or until the pastry is cooked. Leave in the tin for 15 minutes before inverting onto a serving plate.

note *The moisture content of apples varies quite a lot, which affects the cooking time. Golden delicious, pink lady or fuji apples are good to use because they don't break down during cooking.*

raspberry lattice pies

125 g (4½ oz/½ cup) cream cheese
125 g (4½ oz) unsalted butter
185 g (6½ oz/1½ cups) plain (all-purpose) flour
1 egg, beaten
1 tablespoon caster (superfine) sugar

filling

250 g (9 oz/2 cups) raspberries
70 g (3 oz) unsalted butter, softened
90 g (3 oz/⅓ cup) caster (superfine) sugar
1 egg
70 g (3 oz/⅔ cup) ground almonds

makes 8

method   Beat the cream cheese and butter until soft. Stir in the sifted flour with a knife and mix to form a dough. Press together to form a ball. Lightly grease eight small pie dishes or eight 125 ml (4 fl oz/½ cup) muffin holes. Roll out the pastry between two sheets of baking paper until 3 mm (⅛ inch) thick. Cut out eight rounds with a 10 cm (4 inch) cutter and ease into the tins.

Divide the raspberries among the pastry cases. Cream together the butter and sugar and then beat in the egg. Fold in the almonds and spoon on top of the raspberries.

Preheat the oven to 180°C (350°F/Gas 4). Roll out the pastry scraps and cut into 5 mm (¼ inch) wide strips. Weave into a lattice on a board, lightly press down with the palm of your hand and cut into rounds with the 10 cm (4 inch) cutter. Brush the pastry rims of the tartlets with beaten egg, put the lattice rounds on top and gently press down the edges to seal. Re-roll the pastry scraps until the tartlets are all topped. Glaze with beaten egg, sprinkle with caster sugar and bake for 20–25 minutes, or until golden.

apple strudel

4 green cooking apples
30 g (1 oz) butter
2 tablespoons orange juice
1 tablespoon honey
55 g (2 oz/¼ cup) sugar
90 g (3 oz/¾ cup) sultanas (golden raisins)
2 sheets puff pastry
25 g (1 oz/¼ cup) ground almonds
1 egg, lightly beaten
2 tablespoons soft brown sugar
1 teaspoon ground cinnamon

serves 8–10

method Preheat the oven to 220°C (425°F/Gas 7). Lightly grease two oven trays. Peel, core and thinly slice the apples. Heat the butter in a pan and cook the apples for 2 minutes until lightly golden. Add the orange juice, honey, sugar and sultanas and stir until the sugar dissolves and the apples are just tender. Leave to cool completely.

Place a sheet of pastry on a flat work surface. Fold in half and make small cuts in the folded edge at 2 cm (³/₄ inch) intervals. Open out the pastry and sprinkle with half of the ground almonds. Drain the cooked apple and place half of the apple in the centre of the pastry. Brush the edges with egg and fold together, pressing firmly.

Place the strudel on one of the oven trays, seam side down. Brush with egg and sprinkle with half of the combined sugar and cinnamon. Make another strudel with the remaining pastry and apple filling. Bake for 20–25 minutes, or until the pastry is golden and crisp.

variation *Many types of fresh or tinned fruit, such as pears, cherries and apricots, can be used to make strudel.*

lime and blueberry tart

375 g (13 oz) ready-made sweet shortcrust
  pastry
3 eggs
125 g (5 oz/½ cup) caster (superfine) sugar
60 ml (2 fl oz/¼ cup) buttermilk
1 tablespoon lime juice
2 teaspoons finely grated lime zest
2 tablespoons custard powder
250 g (9 oz) blueberries
icing (confectioners') sugar, to serve

serves 8

method   Roll out the pastry between two sheets of baking paper to line a 23 cm (9 inch) pie tin, trimming away the excess pastry. Refrigerate for 20 minutes. Preheat the oven to 200°C (400°F/Gas 6).

Line the pastry with baking paper and spread with baking beads or rice. Bake for 10 minutes, remove the paper and beads and bake for 4–5 minutes, until the pastry is dry. Cool slightly. Reduce the oven to 180°C (350°F/Gas 4).

To make the filling, beat the eggs and caster sugar with electric beaters until thick and pale. Add the buttermilk, lime juice and zest, and sifted custard powder. Stir together, then spoon into the pastry. Bake for 15 minutes, then reduce the oven to 160°C (315°F/Gas 2–3) and cook for 20–25 minutes, or until the filling has coloured slightly and is set. Leave to cool (it will sink a little), then top with the blueberries. Serve sprinkled with icing sugar.

mince pies

250 g (9 oz/2 cups) plain (all-purpose) flour
½ teaspoon ground cinnamon
125 g (4½ oz) unsalted butter, chilled and cubed
1 teaspoon finely grated orange zest
30 g (1 oz/¼ cup) icing (confectioners') sugar, sifted
1 egg yolk
3–4 tablespoons iced water

filling

60 g (2 oz/½ cup) raisins, chopped
60 g (2 oz/⅓ cup) soft brown sugar
40 g (1½ oz/⅓ cup) sultanas (golden raisins)
45 g (1½ oz/¼ cup) mixed peel
1 tablespoon currants
1 tablespoon chopped blanched almonds
1 small green apple, grated
1 teaspoon lemon juice
1 teaspoon finely grated lemon zest
1 teaspoon finely grated orange zest
½ teaspoon mixed (pumpkin pie) spice
¼ teaspoon grated ginger
pinch of ground nutmeg
25 g (1 oz) unsalted butter, melted
1 tablespoon brandy
icing (confectioners') sugar, for dusting

makes 12

method Sift the flour, cinnamon and ¼ teaspoon salt into a large bowl. Rub the butter into the flour with your fingertips until it resembles fine breadcrumbs. Stir in the orange zest and icing sugar. Make a well in the centre and add the egg yolk and most of the water. Mix with a flat-bladed knife, using a cutting action, until the mixture comes together in beads, adding more water if necessary. Gather together, lift onto a lightly floured work surface and press into a disc, wrap in plastic wrap and refrigerate for 20 minutes. Mix together all the filling ingredients.

Preheat the oven to 180°C (350°F/Gas 4). Grease a 12-hole shallow patty pan or mini muffin tin. Roll out two-thirds of the pastry between two sheets of baking paper until 3 mm (⅛ inch) thick. Use an 8 cm (3¼ inch) round biscuit cutter to cut out rounds to line the patty pans.

Divide the filling among the patty cases. Roll out the remaining pastry and cut out 12 rounds with a 7 cm (2¾ inch) cutter. Using a 2.5 cm (1 inch) star cutter, cut a star from the centre of each. Use the outside part to top the tarts, pressing the edges together to seal. Refrigerate for 20 minutes.

Bake for 25 minutes, or until the pastry is golden. Leave in the pan for 5 minutes before cooling on a wire rack. Dust with icing sugar to serve.

note *Any extra fruit mince can be stored in a sterilised jar in a cool, dark place for 3 months.*

pecan pie

185 g (6½ oz/1½ cups) plain (all-purpose) flour
125 g (4½ oz) unsalted butter, chilled
   and cubed
2–3 tablespoons iced water

filling

200 g (7 oz/2 cups) pecans
3 eggs, lightly beaten
50 g (2 oz) unsalted butter, melted
   and cooled
140 g (5 oz/¾ cup) soft brown sugar
170 ml (6 fl oz/⅔ cup) light corn syrup
1 teaspoon natural vanilla extract (essence)
icing (confectioners') sugar, for dusting

serves 6

method Mix the flour and butter in a food processor for 20 seconds or until fine and crumbly. Add almost all the water and process briefly until the mixture comes together, adding a little more water if necessary. Turn out onto a lightly floured surface and gather into a ball.

Roll the pastry out to a large rectangle and line a fluted 35 x 11 cm (14 x 4¼ inch) flan (tart) tin. Chill for 20 minutes.

Preheat the oven to 180°C (350°F/Gas 4). Cover the pastry with baking paper and fill with baking beads or rice. Bake for 15 minutes. Remove the paper and rice and bake for another 10 minutes, or until dry and golden. Cool completely.

Spread pecans over the pastry base. Whisk together the egg, butter, brown sugar, corn syrup, vanilla and a pinch of salt, then pour carefully over the nuts. Decorate with pastry trimmings, then put the tin on an oven tray and bake for 45 minutes. Lightly dust with icing sugar and allow to cool before serving at room temperature.

chocolate tarts

250 g (9 oz/2 cups) plain (all-purpose) flour
2 tablespoons custard powder
125 g (4½ oz) unsalted butter, chilled
and cubed
1 egg yolk
2–3 tablespoons iced water

filling

250 g (9 oz/1 cup) cream cheese,
at room temperature
125 g (5 oz/½ cup) caster (superfine) sugar
1 egg
125 g (5 oz) dark chocolate, melted
25 g (1 oz/¼ cup) ground almonds
100 g (4 oz) white chocolate, melted

makes 24

method Preheat the oven to 180°C (350°F/ Gas 4). Lightly grease two 12-cup shallow patty pans or mini muffin tins. Mix the flour, custard powder and butter in a food processor for 30 seconds, or until fine and crumbly. Add the egg yolk and almost all of the water and process for 20 seconds or until the mixture just comes together, adding the rest of the water if necessary. Turn out onto a lightly floured surface and gather into a smooth ball. Wrap in plastic wrap and refrigerate for 20 minutes.

Divide the dough in half, re-wrap one portion and set aside. Roll the other half between two sheets of baking paper until 3 mm (1/8 inch) thick. Cut out rounds with a 7 cm (2¾ inch) fluted cutter to line the tins. Repeat with the other portion of pastry. Refrigerate both trays while preparing the filling.

Beat the cream cheese and sugar until light and creamy. Add the egg and cooled melted dark chocolate. Beat until there are no streaks visible. Stir in the ground almonds. Spoon the mixture into the pastry cases and bake for 15 minutes, or until just beginning to firm (the filling will set on standing). Cool on a wire rack. Drizzle with the melted white chocolate and leave to set.

orange macadamia tarts

185 g (6½ oz/1½ cups) plain (all-purpose) flour
100 g (3½ oz) unsalted butter
3–4 tablespoons iced water

filling

240 g (8 oz/1½ cups) macadamia nuts
45 g (1½ oz/¼ cup) soft brown sugar
2 tablespoons light corn syrup
20 g (1 oz) unsalted butter, melted
1 egg, lightly beaten
2 teaspoons finely grated orange zest
icing (confectioners') sugar, to serve

makes 6

method Preheat the oven to 180°C (350°F/Gas 4). Spread the nuts on an oven tray and bake for 8 minutes, or until lightly golden. Leave to cool.

Mix the flour and butter in a food processor for 15 seconds, or until fine and crumbly. Add almost all the water and process briefly until the dough just comes together, adding more water if necessary. Turn out onto a lightly floured surface and press together into a smooth ball. Divide the dough into six portions and roll out to line six 8 cm (3¼ inch) fluted flan (tart) tins. Refrigerate the lined tins for 15 minutes.

Line the tins with baking paper and spread with a layer of baking beads or rice. Bake for 15 minutes, then discard the paper and beads. Bake for another 10 minutes, or until the pastry is dry and lightly golden. Cool completely.

Divide the nuts among the tarts. Use a wire whisk to beat together the sugar, corn syrup, butter, egg, orange zest and a pinch of salt. Pour over the nuts and bake for 20 minutes, or until set and lightly browned. Sprinkle with icing sugar to serve.

banana cream pie

375 g (13 oz) ready-made shortcrust pastry
90 g (3 oz/½ cup) dark chocolate chips
4 egg yolks
125 g (5 oz/½ cup) caster (superfine) sugar
½ teaspoon natural vanilla extract (essence)
2 tablespoons custard powder
500 ml (17 fl oz/2 cups) milk
40 g (1½ oz) unsalted butter, softened
1 teaspoon brandy or rum
3 large ripe bananas, thinly sliced, plus extra, to decorate
60 g (2 oz/½ cup) grated dark chocolate

serves 6–8

method Roll out the pastry between two sheets of baking paper to line an 18 cm (7 inch) pie tin, pressing it firmly into the side and trimming away the excess. Refrigerate for 20 minutes.

Preheat the oven to 190°C (375°F/Gas 5). Line the pastry with baking paper and spread with baking beads or rice. Bake for 10 minutes, remove the paper and beads and bake for 10–12 minutes, until the pastry is dry and lightly golden.

While it is hot, place the chocolate chips in the pastry base. Leave for 5 minutes to melt, then spread over the crust with the back of a spoon.

To make the filling, beat the egg yolks, sugar, vanilla extract and custard powder with electric beaters for 2–3 minutes, until pale and thick. Bring the milk to boiling point in a small saucepan, then remove from the heat and gradually pour into the egg and sugar mixture, stirring well. Return to the pan and bring to the boil, stirring. Cook for 2 minutes, or until thickened. Remove from the heat and stir in the butter and brandy. Cool completely.

Arrange the banana over the chocolate, then pour the custard over the top. Refrigerate until ready to serve. Decorate with banana slices and the grated chocolate.

freeform blueberry pie

185 g (6½ oz/1½ cups) plain (all-purpose) flour
100 g (3½ oz) unsalted butter, chilled
    and cubed
2 teaspoons grated orange zest
1 tablespoon caster (superfine) sugar
2–3 tablespoons iced water

filling

40 g (1½ oz/⅓ cup) crushed amaretti biscuits
    or almond bread
60 g (2 oz/½ cup) plain (all-purpose) flour
1 teaspoon ground cinnamon
90 g (3 oz/⅓ cup) caster (superfine) sugar
500 g (1 lb 2 oz/3¼ cups) blueberries
milk, for brushing

serves 6–8

method Sift the flour into a large bowl and rub in the butter with your fingertips until the mixture resembles fine breadcrumbs. Stir in the orange zest and sugar. Make a well in the centre, add almost all the water and mix with a flat-bladed knife, using a cutting action, until the mixture comes together in beads. Add more water if necessary to bring the dough together. Turn out onto a lightly floured surface and gather into a ball. Wrap in plastic wrap and refrigerate for 20 minutes.

Preheat the oven to 200°C (400°F/Gas 6). For the filling, combine the crushed biscuit, flour, cinnamon and 1½ tablespoons sugar. Roll the pastry out to a 36 cm (14 inch) circle and sprinkle with the biscuit mixture, leaving a 4 cm (1½ inch) border. Arrange the blueberries evenly over the biscuit base, then bring up the edges of the pastry to make a crust.

Brush the side of the pie with the milk. Sprinkle with the remaining sugar and bake for 30 minutes, or until the sides are crisp and brown. Serve at room temperature.

mango and passionfruit pies

750 g (1 lb 10 oz) ready-made sweet
shortcrust pastry
3 ripe mangoes, peeled and sliced or chopped,
or 400 g (14 oz) tin mango slices, drained
60 g (2 oz/¼ cup) passionfruit pulp
1 tablespoon custard powder
90 g (3 oz/⅓ cup) caster (superfine) sugar
1 egg, lightly beaten
icing (confectioners') sugar, to dust

makes 6

method Preheat the oven to 190°C (375°F/Gas 5). Grease six 8 cm (3¼ inch) fluted flan (tart) tins. Roll out two-thirds of the pastry between two sheets of baking paper until 3 mm (⅛ inch) thick. Cut out six 13 cm (5 inch) circles. Line the tins with the circles and trim the edges. Refrigerate while you make the filling.

Mix together the mango, passionfruit, custard powder and sugar.

Roll out the remaining pastry between baking paper to 3 mm (⅛ inch) thick and cut out six 11 cm (4¼ inch) circles. Re-roll the trimmings and cut out small shapes for decorations.

Fill the pastry cases with the mango mixture and brush the edges with egg. Top with the pastry circles, press the edges to seal and trim. Decorate with the shapes. Brush the tops with beaten egg and dust with icing sugar. Bake for 20–25 minutes, or until the pastry is golden.

almond pies

30 g (1 oz/⅓ cup) flaked almonds
60 g (2 oz) unsalted butter, softened
60 g (2 oz/½ cup) icing (confectioners') sugar
60 g (2 oz/¾ cup) ground almonds
30 g (1 oz/¼ cup) plain (all-purpose) flour
1 egg
2 teaspoons rum or brandy
¼ teaspoon natural vanilla extract (essence)
4 sheets puff pastry
1 egg, lightly beaten
1 tablespoon sugar

makes 8

method Preheat the oven to 200°C (400°F/Gas 6). Toast the flaked almonds on a baking tray for 2–3 minutes, or until just golden. Remove the almonds and return the tray to the oven to keep it hot.

Beat together the butter, icing sugar, ground almonds, flour, eggs, rum and vanilla with electric beaters for 2–3 minutes, until smooth and combined. Fold in the flaked almonds.

Cut out eight 10 cm (4 inch) rounds and eight 11 cm (4¼ inch) rounds from the pastry. Spread the smaller rounds with the filling, leaving a small border. Brush the borders with beaten egg and cover with the tops. Seal the edges with a fork. Pierce the tops to make steam holes. Brush with egg and sprinkle with sugar. Bake on the hot tray for 15–20 minutes, or until the pastry is puffed and golden.

honey and pine nut tart

250 g (9 oz/2 cups) plain (all-purpose) flour
1½ tablespoons icing (confectioners') sugar
115 g (4 oz) unsalted butter, chilled and cubed
1 egg, lightly beaten
2 tablespoons iced water

filling

235 g (8 oz/1½ cups) pine nuts
180 g (6 oz/½ cup) honey
115 g (4 oz) unsalted butter, softened
125 g (5 oz/½ cup) caster (superfine) sugar
3 eggs, lightly beaten
¼ teaspoon natural vanilla extract (essence)
1 tablespoon almond liqueur
1 teaspoon finely grated lemon zest
1 tablespoon lemon juice
icing (confectioners') sugar, for dusting

serves 6

method Preheat the oven to 190°C (375°F/Gas 5). Place a baking tray on the middle shelf. Lightly grease a 23 x 3.5 cm (9 x 1½ inch) deep loose-based flan (tart) tin. Sift the flour and icing sugar into a bowl. Rub in the butter with your fingertips until the mixture resembles fine breadcrumbs. Make a well in the centre and add the egg and water. Mix with a flat-bladed knife, using a cutting action, until the dough comes together in beads.

Turn out onto a lightly floured work surface and press together into a ball. Roll out to a circle 3 mm (1/8 inch) thick to line the tin and trim away any excess pastry. Prick the base all over with a fork and chill for 15 minutes. Cut out leaves from the trimmings for decoration. Cover and chill.

Line the pastry with baking paper and spread with a layer of baking beads or rice. Bake on the heated tray for 10 minutes, then remove.

Reduce the oven to 180°C (350°F/Gas 4). Spread the pine nuts on a baking tray and roast in the oven for 3 minutes, or until golden. Heat the honey in a small saucepan until runny. Beat the butter and sugar in a bowl until smooth and pale. Gradually add the egg, a little at a time, beating well after each addition. Mix in the honey, vanilla, liqueur, lemon zest and juice and a pinch of salt. Stir in the pine nuts, spoon into the pastry case and smooth the surface. Arrange the pastry leaves in the centre.

Place on the hot tray and bake for 40 minutes, or until golden and set. Cover the top with foil after 25 minutes. Serve warm, dusted with icing sugar, perhaps with crème fraîche or mascarpone cheese.

low-fat banana and blueberry tart

125 g (4½ oz/1 cup) plain (all-purpose) flour
60 g (2 oz/½ cup) self-raising flour
1 teaspoon ground cinnamon
1 teaspoon ground ginger
40 g (1½ oz) unsalted butter, chilled and cubed
95 g (3 oz ½ cup) soft brown sugar
125 ml (4 fl oz/½ cup) buttermilk
200 g (7 oz/1¼ cups) blueberries
2 bananas
2 teaspoons lemon juice
1 tablespoon raw (demerara) sugar
icing (confectioners') sugar, to serve

serves 6–8

method   Preheat the oven to 200°C (400°F/Gas 6). Lightly grease a baking tray or pizza tray. Sift the flours and spices into a bowl. Add the butter and sugar and rub in until the mixture resembles fine breadcrumbs. Make a well in the centre and add enough buttermilk to mix to a soft dough.

Roll the dough on a lightly floured surface into a 23 cm (9 inch) circle. Place on the tray and roll the edge into a lip to hold in the fruit.

Spread the blueberries over the dough. Slice the bananas, toss them in the lemon juice, and arrange over the top. Sprinkle with the sugar, and bake for 25 minutes, until the base is browned. Dust with icing sugar and serve immediately.

summer berry tart

125 g (4½ oz/1 cup) plain (all-purpose) flour
90 g (3 oz) unsalted butter, chilled and cubed
2 tablespoons icing (confectioners') sugar
1–2 tablespoons iced water

filling

3 egg yolks
2 tablespoons caster (superfine) sugar
2 tablespoons cornflour (cornstarch)
250 ml (9 oz/1 cup) milk
1 teaspoon natural vanilla extract (essence)
250 g (9 oz) strawberries, hulled and halved
125 g (5 oz) blueberries
125 g (5 oz) raspberries
1–2 tablespoons redcurrant jelly

serves 4–6

method Mix the flour, butter and icing sugar in a food processor for 15 seconds, or until fine and crumbly. Add enough of the water to make the dough just come together. Turn onto a lightly floured surface and shape into a ball. Roll out to line a 20 cm (8 inch) fluted flan (tart) tin, trimming away the excess. Refrigerate for 20 minutes. Preheat oven to 180°C (350°F/Gas 4).

Line the tin with baking paper and a layer of baking beads or rice and bake for 15 minutes. Remove the paper and beads and bake for another 15 minutes, until dry and lightly golden.

Whisk the egg yolks, sugar and cornflour until pale. Heat the milk in a small pan to almost boiling, then pour gradually into the egg mixture, beating constantly. Strain back into the pan. Stir over low heat for 3 minutes or until the custard boils and thickens. Remove from the heat and add the vanilla. Transfer to a bowl, lay plastic wrap directly on the surface to prevent a skin forming, and leave to cool.

Spread the custard in the pastry shell and top with the strawberries, blueberries and raspberries. Heat the redcurrant jelly until liquid and brush over the fruit.

passionfruit tart

125 g (4½ oz/1 cup) plain (all-purpose) flour
45 g (1½ oz/¼ cup) ground almonds
60 g (2 oz/¼ cup) caster (superfine) sugar
60 g (2 oz) unsalted butter, chilled and cubed
2–3 tablespoons iced water

filling

6 egg yolks
125 g (5 oz/½ cup) caster (superfine) sugar
185 g (7 oz/¾ cup) passionfruit pulp
75 g (3 oz) unsalted butter
1½ teaspoons gelatine
125 ml (4 fl oz/½ cup) cream, whipped

serves 8

method Preheat the oven to 180°C (350°F/Gas 4). Mix the flour, ground almonds, sugar and butter in a food processor for 30 seconds or until fine and crumbly. Add almost all the water and process for another 30 seconds or until the dough just comes together (add more water if necessary). Turn onto a lightly floured surface and press together into a smooth ball.

Roll out the pastry to fit a 23 cm (9 inch) fluted flan (tart) tin, trimming away the excess. Refrigerate for 20 minutes. Cover with baking paper and spread with a layer of baking beads or rice. Bake for 15 minutes, then discard the paper and beads. Bake for another 15 minutes, until the pastry is lightly golden and dry. Cool completely.

Whisk the yolks and sugar in a heatproof bowl for 1 minute or until slightly thickened and pale. Stir in the passionfruit pulp. Stand the bowl over a pan of simmering water and stir gently but constantly for 15 minutes, adding the butter gradually until the mixture thickens. Remove from the heat and cool slightly.

Put the gelatine in a small bowl with 1 tablespoon water. Leave until spongy, then stir until dissolved. Stir thoroughly into the passionfruit filling. Cool to room temperature, stirring occasionally. Fold in the whipped cream. Spread into the pastry shell and smooth the surface. Keep chilled until ready to serve.

storage *Keep the tart refrigerated until you are ready to serve.*

plum cobbler

750 g (1 lb 10 oz) plums
90 g (3 oz/⅓ cup) sugar
1 teaspoon natural vanilla extract (essence)

topping

125 g (5 oz/1 cup) self-raising flour
60 g (2 oz) unsalted butter, chilled and cubed
60 g (2 oz/⅓ cup) soft brown sugar
60 ml (2 fl oz/¼ cup) milk
1 tablespoon caster (superfine) sugar

serves 6

method   Preheat the oven to 200°C (400°F/Gas 6). Cut the plums into quarters and then remove the stones. Put the plums, sugar and 2 tablespoons water in a saucepan and bring to the boil, stirring, until the sugar dissolves.

Reduce the heat, then cover and simmer for 5 minutes, or until the plums are tender. Remove the skins if you prefer. Add the vanilla and spoon the mixture into a 750 ml (26 fl oz/3 cup) ovenproof dish.

To make the topping, sift the flour into a bowl and add the butter. Rub in the butter with your fingertips until the mixture resembles fine breadcrumbs. Stir in the brown sugar and 2 tablespoons of the milk. Stir with a knife to form a soft dough, adding more milk if necessary.

Turn out onto a lightly floured surface and gather together to form a smooth dough. Roll out until 1 cm (½ inch) thick and cut into rounds with a 4 cm (1½ inch) cutter.

Overlap the rounds around the inside edge of the dish over the filling. Lightly brush with milk and sprinkle with sugar. Bake on a tray for 30 minutes, or until the topping is golden and cooked through.

lemon meringue pie

375 g (13 oz) sweet shortcrust pastry
30 g (1 oz/¼ cup) plain (all-purpose) flour
30 g (1 oz/¼ cup) cornflour (cornstarch)
230 g (8 oz/1 cup) caster (superfine) sugar
185 ml (6 fl oz/¾ cup) lemon juice
1 tablespoon grated lemon zest
50 g (2 oz) unsalted butter, chopped
6 egg yolks

meringue

4 egg whites
345 g (12 oz/1 cup) caster (superfine) sugar
pinch of cream of tartar

serves 6–8

method Lightly grease an 18 cm (7 inch) pie plate. Roll out the pastry between two sheets of baking paper into a 30 cm (12 inch) circle to line the pie plate, and trim away the excess. Press a teaspoon into the pastry rim to make a decorative edge. Prick all over the base with a fork. Cover and refrigerate for 20 minutes. Preheat the oven to 180°C (350°F/Gas 4).

Line the pastry with baking paper and spread with a layer of baking beads or rice. Bake for 15 minutes, then remove the paper and beads and bake for 15–20 minutes, or until the pastry is dry. Leave to cool. Increase the oven to 200°C (400°F/Gas 6).

To make the lemon filling, put the flours, sugar, lemon juice and zest in a saucepan. Gradually add 310 ml (11 fl oz/1¼ cups) water and whisk over medium heat until smooth. Cook, stirring, for another 2 minutes, or until thickened. Remove from the heat and vigorously whisk in the butter and egg yolks. Return to low heat and stir for 2 minutes, or until the filling is very thick.

To make the meringue, in a clean, dry bowl beat the egg whites, sugar and cream of tartar with electric beaters for 10 minutes, until thick and glossy.

Spread the lemon filling over the cooled pastry base, then spread the meringue over the top, piling it high in the centre. Use a knife to form peaks in the meringue. Bake for 12–15 minutes, or until the meringue is lightly browned.

cherry pie

150 g (5½ oz/1¼ cups) plain (all-purpose) flour
30 g (1 oz/¼ cup) icing (confectioners') sugar
60 g (2 oz) ground almonds
100 g (3½ oz) unsalted butter, chilled
and cubed
60 ml (2 fl oz/¼ cup) iced water
2 x 700 g (1 lb 9 oz) tins pitted morello
cherries, drained
1 egg, lightly beaten
caster (superfine) sugar, to sprinkle

serves 6–8

method   Sift the flour and icing sugar into a bowl and then stir in the ground almonds. Rub in the butter with your fingertips until the mixture resembles fine breadcrumbs. Add almost all the water and cut into the flour mixture with a flat-bladed knife until the mixture forms beads, adding the remaining water if necessary.

Turn the dough out onto a lightly floured surface and press together until smooth. Roll out the dough to a 25 cm (10 inch) circle. Cover with plastic and refrigerate for about 15 minutes.

Preheat the oven to 200°C (400°F/Gas 6). Spoon the cherries into a 23 cm (9 inch) round pie dish. Cover the pie dish with the pastry top and trim away the excess. Roll out the trimmings to make decorations. Brush the pastry top with beaten egg to secure the decorations and sprinkle lightly with caster sugar. Place the pie dish on baking tray and bake for 35–40 minutes, or until golden.

portuguese custard tarts

150 g (5½ oz/1¼ cups) plain (all-purpose) flour
25 g (1 oz) white vegetable shortening, softened
30 g (1 oz) unsalted butter, softened
250 g (9 oz/1 cup) sugar
500 ml (17 fl oz/2 cups) milk
30 g (1 oz/¼ cup) cornflour (cornstarch)
1 tablespoon custard powder
4 egg yolks
1 teaspoon natural vanilla extract (essence)

makes 12

method   Sift the flour into a large bowl and add about 185 ml (6 fl oz/³/₄ cup) water, or enough to form a soft dough. Gather together, then roll out on baking paper into a 24 x 30 cm (9¹/₂ x 12 inch) rectangle. Spread with the vegetable shortening. Roll up from the short edge to form a log.

Roll the dough out into a rectangle once again, and spread with the butter. Roll up into a log and slice into 12 even-sized pieces. Working from the centre, use your fingertips to press out each round until large enough to line twelve 80 ml (2¹/₂ fl oz/¹/₃ cup) muffin holes. Refrigerate tins.

Put the sugar and 80 ml (2¹/₂ fl oz/¹/₃ cup) water in a saucepan and stir over low heat until the sugar dissolves.

Mix a little of the milk with the cornflour and custard powder to form a smooth paste, and add to the sugar syrup with the remaining milk, egg yolks and vanilla. Stir over low heat until thickened. Place in a bowl, then cover and cool.

Preheat the oven to 220°C (425°F/Gas 7). Divide the custard filling among the muffin holes and bake for 25–30 minutes, or until the custard is set and the tops have browned. Cool in the tins, then transfer to a wire rack.

nutty fig pie

375 g (13 oz) ready-made sweet
shortcrust pastry
200 g (7 oz/1½ cups) hazelnuts
100 g (4 oz/⅔ cup) pine nuts
100 g (4 oz/heaped 1 cup) flaked almonds
100 g (4 oz/⅔ cup) blanched almonds
150 ml (5 fl oz) cream
60 g (2 oz) unsalted butter
90 g (3 oz/¼ cup) honey
95 g (3 oz/½ cup) soft brown sugar
150 g (5 oz) dessert figs, quartered

serves 8

method Preheat the oven to 200°C (400°F/Gas 6) and grease a 20 cm (8 inch) pie tin. Roll the pastry out between two sheets of baking paper until large enough to line the tin, trimming away the excess. Use a fork to prick the base several times and score the edge. Refrigerate for 20 minutes, then bake for 15 minutes, or until dry and lightly golden. Allow to cool.

Meanwhile, bake the hazelnuts on a baking tray for 8 minutes, or until the skins start to peel away. Tip the hot nuts into a tea towel (dish towel) and rub to remove the skins. Put the pine nuts, flaked almonds and blanched almonds on a baking tray and bake for 5–6 minutes, or until lightly golden.

Place the cream, butter, honey and brown sugar in a saucepan and stir over medium heat until the sugar dissolves and the butter melts. Remove from the heat and stir in the nuts and figs. Spoon into the pastry case and bake for 30 minutes, or until the pastry is golden and the filling is set. Remove and allow to cool before slicing.

pear and apple crumble pie

375 g (13 oz) ready-made shortcrust pastry
3 pears
4 green apples
60 g (2 oz/¼ cup) caster (superfine) sugar
2 teaspoons grated orange zest
90 g (3 oz/¾ cup) raisins
60 g (2 oz/¼ cup) plain (all-purpose) flour
60 g (2 oz/¼ cup) soft brown sugar
½ teaspoon ground ginger
60 g (2 oz) unsalted butter

serves 8

method Roll out the pastry between two sheets of baking paper until large enough to line an 18 cm (7 inch) pie dish, trimming away the excess. Wrap in plastic wrap and refrigerate for 20 minutes.

Meanwhile, peel, core and slice the pears and apples and place in a large saucepan. Add the caster sugar, orange zest and 2 tablespoons water and cook over low heat, stirring occasionally for 20 minutes, or until the fruit is tender but still holding its shape. Remove from the heat, add the raisins and a pinch of salt, mix and leave to cool completely. Spoon into the pie dish.

Preheat the oven to 200°C (400°F/Gas 6) and preheat a baking tray. To make the topping, put the flour, brown sugar and ginger in a bowl and rub in the butter with your fingertips until the mixture resembles coarse breadcrumbs. Sprinkle over the fruit.

Put the dish on the hot baking tray and bake for 10 minutes, then reduce the oven temperature to 180°C (350°F/Gas 4) and bake for another 40 minutes, or until browned. Check the pie after 20 minutes and cover with foil if the topping is over-browning.

filo peach tartlets

6 sheets filo pastry
60 g (2 oz) unsalted butter, melted
90 g (3 oz/¾ cup) slivered almonds
1½ teaspoons ground cinnamon
90 g (3 oz/½ cup) soft brown sugar
185 ml (6 fl oz/¾ cup) orange juice, strained
4 peaches

makes 8

method Preheat the oven to 180°C (350°F/Gas 4). Cut each sheet of pastry into eight squares. Line eight large muffin holes with three layers of filo pastry, brushing between layers with melted butter and overlapping the sheets at angles.

Mix together the almonds, cinnamon and half the sugar. Sprinkle into the pastry cases, then cover with three final squares of filo brushed with butter. Bake for 10–15 minutes.

Meanwhile, dissolve the remaining sugar in the orange juice in a saucepan, bring to the boil, reduce the heat and simmer. Halve the peaches and slice thinly. Add to the syrup and stir gently to coat the fruit. Simmer for 2–3 minutes then lift from the pan with a slotted spoon. Arrange the peaches on the pastries and serve.

variation *You can use tinned peaches if fresh are not available.*

apple pie

6 large green apples, peeled, cored and
   cut into wedges
2 tablespoons caster (superfine) sugar
1 teaspoon finely grated lemon zest
pinch of ground cloves
2 tablespoons apricot jam
1 egg, lightly beaten
1 tablespoon sugar

pastry

310 g (11 oz/2½ cups) plain (all-purpose) flour
40 g (1½ oz/⅓ cup) self-raising flour
185 g (6½ oz) butter, chilled and cubed
2½ tablespoons caster (superfine) sugar
120–140 ml (4–5 fl oz) iced water

serves 6–8

method · Put the apples in a large heavy-based saucepan with the sugar, lemon zest, cloves and 2 tablespoons water. Cover and simmer for 8 minutes, or until just tender, shaking the pan occasionally. Drain and cool.

To make the pastry, sift the flours into a bowl. Rub the butter into the flour with your fingertips until the mixture resembles fine breadcrumbs. Add the sugar, mix well and make a well in the centre. Add most of the water and mix with a flat-bladed knife, using a cutting action, until the mixture just comes together in beads, adding water if needed. Gather the pastry together on a floured surface. Divide into two, making one half a little bigger. Wrap in plastic and refrigerate for 20 minutes.

Preheat the oven to 200°C (400°F/Gas 6). Roll out the larger piece of pastry between two sheets of baking paper and line a 23 cm (9 inch) pie plate, trimming away the excess pastry. Brush the jam over the base and spoon in the apple filling. Roll out the remaining piece of pastry between two sheets of baking paper until large enough to cover the pie. Brush a little water around the rim to secure the top. Trim off the excess pastry, pinch the edges together and cut steam holes in the top.

Roll out the trimmings to make leaves to decorate the pie. Brush the top lightly with egg and sprinkle with sugar. Bake for 20 minutes, then reduce the oven temperature to 180°C (350°F/Gas 4) and bake for 30–35 minutes, or until golden brown.

date and mascarpone tart

90 g (3 oz/½ cup) rice flour
60 g (2 oz/½ cup) plain (all-purpose) flour
2 tablespoons icing (confectioners') sugar
25 g (1 oz/¼ cup) desiccated coconut
100 g (3½ oz) marzipan, chopped
100 g (3½ oz) unsalted butter, chilled
and cubed

filling

200 g (7 oz) fresh dates, stones removed
2 eggs
2 teaspoons custard powder
125 g (5 oz) mascarpone cheese
2 tablespoons caster (superfine) sugar
80 ml (3 fl oz/⅓ cup) cream
2 tablespoons flaked almonds
icing (confectioners') sugar, to serve

serves 6–8

method Preheat the oven to 180°C (350°F/Gas 4) and grease a shallow 35 x 10 cm (14 x 4 inch) fluted loose-based flan (tart) tin.

Mix the flours, icing sugar, coconut and marzipan in a food processor for 10 seconds. Add the butter and mix for 10–20 seconds, or until the dough just comes together when squeezed (do not over-process). Turn out onto a lightly floured surface and gather into a ball. Wrap in plastic and refrigerate for 15 minutes.

Cut the dates into quarters lengthways. Roll out the pastry between two sheets of baking paper until large enough to line the tin, trimming away the excess. Refrigerate for another 5–10 minutes. Cover the pastry-lined tin with baking paper and spread with a layer of baking beads or rice. Place the tin on an oven tray and bake for 10 minutes. Remove from the oven and discard the paper and beads. Return to the oven and bake for another 5 minutes or until just golden. Leave to cool.

Arrange the dates over the pastry base. Whisk together the eggs, custard powder, mascarpone, sugar and cream until smooth. Pour over the dates and sprinkle with flaked almonds. Bake for 25–30 minutes, or until golden and just set. Dust with icing sugar and serve immediately, while still hot from the oven.

raspberry shortcake

125 g (4½ oz/1 cup) plain (all-purpose) flour
40 g (1½ oz/⅓ cup) icing (confectioners') sugar
90 g (3 oz) unsalted butter, chilled and cubed
1 egg yolk
½ teaspoon natural vanilla extract (essence)

topping

750 g (1 lb 10 oz) fresh raspberries
3–4 tablespoons icing (confectioners') sugar,
    to taste
100 g (4 oz/⅓ cup) redcurrant jelly

serves 8

method Put the flour, icing sugar and butter in a food processor and process for 15 seconds, or until the mixture is crumbly. Process for 10 seconds, adding the egg yolk, vanilla and enough cold water (about ½–1 tablespoon) to make the dough just come together. Turn out onto a lightly floured surface and gather together into a ball. Wrap in plastic wrap and refrigerate for 30 minutes.

Preheat the oven to 180°C (350°F/Gas 4). Roll out the pastry to fit a fluted 20 cm (8 inch) loose-based flan (tart) tin and trim the edges. Prick all over with a fork and refrigerate for 20 minutes. Bake the pastry for 15–20 minutes, or until golden. Cool on a wire rack.

To make the topping, set aside 500 g (1 lb 2 oz) of the best raspberries and mash the rest with the icing sugar, to taste. Spread the mashed raspberries over the shortcake just before serving. Cover with the whole raspberries.

Heat the redcurrant jelly until liquid in a small saucepan and brush over the raspberries with a soft brush. Slice and serve.

variation You can use 800 g (1 lb 12 oz) frozen raspberries. Thaw in the packet overnight in the fridge and only use when ready to serve.

banoffie pie

150 g (5½ oz/1¼ cups) plain (all-purpose) flour
2 tablespoons icing (confectioners') sugar
90 g (3 oz/¾ cup) ground walnuts
80 g (3 oz) unsalted butter, chilled
and cubed
2–3 tablespoons iced water

filling

400 g (14 oz) tin condensed milk
30 g (1 oz) unsalted butter
1 tablespoon golden syrup (if unavailable, use
half honey and half dark corn syrup)
4 bananas, sliced
375 ml (13 fl oz/1½ cups) cream, for whipping

serves 8

method Sift the flour and icing sugar into a large bowl. Add the walnuts. Rub in the butter until the mixture resembles fine breadcrumbs. Mix in the water with a knife until the dough just comes together. Turn out onto a lightly floured surface and press together into a ball. Wrap in plastic wrap and chill for 15 minutes. Roll out until large enough to line a 23 cm (9 inch) fluted flan (tart) tin, trimming away the excess. Refrigerate for 20 minutes.

Preheat the oven to 180°C (350°F/Gas 4). Cover the pastry with baking paper and spread with a layer of baking beads or rice. Bake for 15 minutes, then remove the paper and beads. Bake the pastry for another 20 minutes, or until dry and lightly golden. Leave to cool completely.

Heat the condensed milk, butter and golden syrup in a small saucepan for 5 minutes, stirring constantly until it boils, thickens and turns a light caramel colour. Cool slightly. Arrange half the banana over the pastry and pour the caramel over the top. Refrigerate for 30 minutes.

Whip the cream and spoon over the caramel. Top with more banana before serving.

farmhouse rhubarb pie

185 g (6½ oz/1½ cups) plain (all-purpose) flour, sifted
125 g (4½ oz) unsalted butter, chilled and cubed
2 tablespoons icing (confectioners') sugar
1 egg yolk
1 tablespoon iced water

filling

250 g (9 oz/1 cup) sugar
750 g (1 lb 10 oz) chopped rhubarb
2 large apples, peeled, cored and chopped
2 teaspoons grated lemon zest
3 pieces preserved ginger, sliced
2 teaspoons sugar
sprinkle of ground cinnamon

serves 6

method   Mix the flour, butter and icing sugar in a food processor until crumbly. Add the yolk and water and process until the dough comes together. Wrap in plastic wrap and refrigerate for 15 minutes.

Preheat the oven to 190°C (375°F/Gas 5). Roll out the pastry to a rough 35 cm (14 inch) circle and line a greased 20 cm (8 inch) pie plate, leaving the extra pastry to hang over the edge. Refrigerate while you prepare the filling.

Heat the sugar with 125 ml (4 fl oz/½ cup) water in a pan for 4–5 minutes, or until syrupy. Add the rhubarb, apple, lemon zest and ginger. Cover and simmer for 5 minutes, until the rhubarb is cooked but still holds its shape.

Drain off the liquid and cool the rhubarb. Spoon into the pastry base and sprinkle with the sugar and cinnamon. Fold the overhanging pastry roughly over the fruit and bake for 40 minutes, or until golden.

golden pine nut tarts

60 g (2 oz/½ cup) plain (all-purpose) flour
60 g (2 oz) unsalted butter, chilled and cubed
40 g (1½ oz/¼ cup) pine nuts
20 g (1 oz) unsalted butter, melted
180 g (6 oz/½ cup) golden syrup
(if unavailable, substitute with half honey
and half dark corn syrup)
2 tablespoons soft brown sugar

makes 24

method Preheat the oven to 180°C (350°F/Gas 4) and brush two 12-hole patty pans or mini muffin tins with melted butter.

Mix the flour and butter in a food processor for 20–30 seconds or until the mixture comes together. Turn onto a lightly floured surface and press into a smooth ball. Roll out to a thickness of 3 mm (⅛ inch). Cut out rounds with a 5 cm (2 inch) fluted scone cutter. Lift rounds gently with a flat-bladed knife and line each muffin hole. Spread the pine nuts on a baking tray and toast in the oven for 1–2 minutes, until just golden. Cool a little, then divide among the pastry cases.

Whisk together the melted butter, syrup and sugar. Pour over the pine nuts. Bake for 15 minutes, until golden. Leave the tarts in the trays for 5 minutes before cooling on a wire rack.

Published in 2010 by Bay Books,
an imprint of Murdoch Books Pty Limited.

Murdoch Books Australia
Pier 8/9,
23 Hickson Road,
Millers Point NSW 2000
Phone: +61 (0)2 8220 2000
Fax: +61 (0)2 8220 2558
www.murdochbooks.com.au

Murdoch Books UK Limited
Erico House, 6th Floor
93–99 Upper Richmond Road
Putney, London SW15 2TG
Phone: + 44 (0) 20 8785 5995
Fax: + 44 (0) 20 8785 5985
www.murdochbooks.co.uk

Chief Executive: Juliet Rogers

Publisher: Lynn Lewis
Senior Designer: Heather Menzies
Designer: Pinch Me Design
Editor: Justine Harding
Editorial Coordinator: Liz Malcolm
Index: Jo Rudd
Production: Alexandra Gonzalez

National Library of Australia Cataloguing-in-Publication Data:
Title: Pies and tarts.
ISBN: 978-1-74266-007-3 (pbk.)
Series: 100 easy recipes.
Notes: Includes index.
Subjects: Pies. Pastry.
641.8652

Printed C & C Offset Printing Co. Ltd. PRINTED IN CHINA.

IMPORTANT: Those who might be at risk from the effects of salmonella poisoning (the elderly, pregnant women, young children and those suffering from immune deficiency diseases) should consult their doctor with any concerns about eating raw eggs.